THE COMPLETE
DOLLS' HOUSE BOOK

THE COMPLETE
DOLLS' HOUSE BOOK

JEAN NISBETT

GUILD OF MASTER CRAFTSMAN PUBLICATIONS LTD

FIRST PUBLISHED 1993 BY
GUILD OF MASTER CRAFTSMAN PUBLICATIONS LTD,
166 HIGH STREET, LEWES,
EAST SUSSEX BN7 1XU

© JEAN NISBETT 1993
REPRINTED 1994

ISBN 0 946819 44 0

DESIGNED BY TERESA DEARLOVE

PRINTED AND BOUND IN SINGAPORE
UNDER THE SUPERVISION OF MRM GRAPHICS, WINSLOW, BUCKINGHAMSHIRE, UK

ACKNOWLEDGEMENTS

I am indebted to the many craftspeople who have contributed photographs of their work, and to countless others whose dolls' houses and miniatures first stimulated my interest. Without them this book would never have been written.

I would also like to thank Joanna Lorenz for her original suggestion and encouragement; my editor, Elizabeth Inman, for her sterling work in bringing the project to fruition; and my husband for the many hours he has spent taking photographs of some of the dolls' houses I have decorated and furnished.

CONTENTS

PART 1   THE HOUSE

PART 2   ACHIEVING THE AUTHENTIC LOOK

PART 3   OTHER THEMES

PART 4   PRACTICAL

FURTHER INFORMATION

INTRODUCTION

THE DINING ROOM OF THIS EXQUISITE HOUSE CONTAINS THE ONLY KNOWN EXAMPLE IN A DOLLS' HOUSE OF HAND-PAINTED WALLPAPER PANELS IN THE CLASSIC LANDSCAPE STYLE POPULAR IN THE EIGHTEENTH CENTURY. THE CHINESE WALLPAPERS IN THE BEDROOMS ARE ALSO BASED ON CONTEMPORARY FASHION. THE SASH WINDOWS CAN BE OPENED, AND THE FESTOON CURTAINS ARE TYPICAL OF THE TIME.
NOTE THE ROASTING JACK ON THE SIDE OF THE KITCHEN CHIMNEYPIECE COMPLETE WITH PULLEY, WEIGHT AND CHAIN TO TURN THE SPIT.

A dolls' house in a museum, exhibition or shop window always attracts attention. Everyone stops to look, to marvel at the scale of the furniture and the minuteness of detail. It is frustrating to see one on display with the front firmly closed, and to be unable to see what is inside.

1

A DELIGHTFUL HOUSE MADE IN 1811 FOR LADY CHARLOTTE THYNNE, WHO LEFT IT AT LONGLEAT WHEN SHE MARRIED. THE STRONG COLOURS REFLECT THE DECORATIVE STYLE OF THE REGENCY PERIOD, AND THE CURVING CHIPPENDALE-STYLE STAIRCASE IS AN ARRESTING CENTREPIECE.
THE HOUSE WAS WELL USED, AND THERE ARE A NUMBER OF HOME-MADE ITEMS AMONG THE GRANDER PIECES. AS WELL AS A SUITE OF IVORY BEDROOM FURNITURE AND A LIBRARY OF 300 BOOKS (ALL FAKE), THERE ARE MANY ORIGINAL DOLLS. HOME-MADE FURNISHINGS INCLUDE TWO FOOT CUSHIONS WORKED BY A LITTLE GIRL IN 1804, AND A COMMODE MADE IN 1835 BY A SMALL BOY NAMED EDWARD.

Dolls' houses and miniatures have been collected and admired since the seventeenth century, when the first 'cabinet houses' were commissioned in the Netherlands for wealthy collectors. From the outside they did not look like today's dolls' houses: the rooms were set into handsome cabinets made by craftsmen to blend in with other furniture, but fitted with glass doors so that the exquisite contents could be seen and admired.

Eighteenth-century English dolls' houses were magnificent creations. They are correctly termed 'baby houses', as the word 'baby' was used at the time to mean 'doll'. They were treasure troves filled with tiny copies of the furniture and fittings present in the grand homes of the owners for whom they were designed. An example in the Museum of London reflects in miniature the arrangement, equipment and decor of a wealthy household of the 1740s, but still manages to look lived in and has all the comfortable clutter of a real home.

In the nineteenth century dolls' houses had gone out of fashion as an adult hobby, and were now intended to be played with by children. The Marquess of Bath is the owner of two dolls' houses which can be seen at Longleat in Wiltshire, one made in 1811 and the other in 1870. These houses are nearer to the modern idea of a dolls' house; both are beautifully made, and the contents are a delight.

In the well-to-do Victorian household there was usually a dolls' house in the nursery. Some were handmade, but by this time dolls' houses were

REPRODUCED BY PERMISSION OF THE MARQUESS OF BATH,
LONGLEAT HOUSE, WARMINSTER, WILTSHIRE.

available in toyshops, together with furniture imported from Germany. The young Princess Victoria owned a plain, commercially made dolls' house, which can still be seen at Kensington Palace in London. Royal interest in dolls' houses went a stage further with Queen Mary's enjoyment in decorating and furnishing miniature rooms which reflected the living arrangements of upper-class houses of the time.

It was not until many years later that interest in dolls' houses and miniatures again became an adult hobby. Queen Mary's dolls' house, the wonderful palace designed and built by Sir Edwin Lutyens and completed in 1924, was furnished with the work of the leading craftsmen of the day. It was, and still is, admired for the richness of its exquisite contents and the glimpse it allowed of the lifestyle of a Royal home, but it lacked that indefinable feeling of being inhabited that might have inspired others to make their own miniature homes – it was too perfect to emulate.

Today's miniaturist usually wants to recreate a lived-in home of some favoured period. Few want to create a replica of a modern home; it is the past that lends enchantment. In each era a particular period has been favoured for reproduction in interior decoration. The Georgians favoured Greek and Roman grandeur. At the time of the Regency, exotic Egyptian, Indian and Chinese styles were copied, and this fashion was followed by a brief flirtation with a frilly version of Gothic, now characterized as 'Gothick'.

The Victorians were heavily into a gloomier Gothic, but William Morris led the revival of mediaeval-style furnishings and the simple life in the late nineteenth century. In the early twentieth century, Tudor, then Regency and again Tudor became favoured periods for the interior decorator to reproduce, and now the country house look is also popular, as it gives an illusion of calm and stability.

The joy of decorating and furnishing a dolls' house is that you can do anything you like, without the restrictions of the real world. There are two

THE AMERICAN SHAKER STYLE IS NOTED FOR ITS NEATNESS AND SIMPLICITY, WHICH IS AS APPROPRIATE IN A MODERN INTERIOR AS IT IS IN A COUNTRY COTTAGE. THIS AUTHENTIC ROOM SETTING SHOWS PRACTICAL FURNITURE FOR EVERYDAY USE AND A SPACE-SAVING STORAGE SYSTEM WHICH IS PERHAPS EVEN MORE RELEVANT TODAY THAN IN THE EIGHTEENTH CENTURY. THE MINIATURE PIECES ARE MADE IN CHERRYWOOD, LIKE THE ORIGINALS; THE MAKER HAS USED THE SHAKER METHODS OF JOINTING WHEREVER POSSIBLE IN SUCH A SMALL SIZE.

PHOTOS COURTESY OF SIMPLY SHAKER.

basic approaches. One is to create an authentic interior with complete architectural accuracy and no compromise on the choices of design and furniture. This is a valid option, and many of today's miniaturists create room settings so perfect as to make us gasp with admiration.

An alternative approach is to create a 'lived-in' home. While it is important that periods should be followed through and that the rooms should in general match the style of the house, people living in real period houses furnish them with a mixture of antiques, inherited items and pieces chosen because they happen to like them, as well as modern equipment. If you choose to reflect real life and not just a particular period, it is permissible to include some anachronisms.

People are not tidy; living itself creates a certain amount of chaos. Rooms need to look as if they are used, otherwise they can create the static ambience of a designer showroom. I like to have families in my houses, and suit the contents to their imagined characters. It is not essential to include dolls: the occupants may have gone out for a moment or be in another room, but there will be traces of their presence – a book left on a chair, some knitting in a corner, painting or writing materials in the study, and children's toys left on the nursery floor.

Today's craftspeople rival and often surpass those of the past. For the collector who can afford them, miniature treasures are being made now which will become heirlooms to be handed on to future generations. The pleasure of owning a dolls' house is to be able to collect or make furniture of the period you enjoy most, without the limitations imposed in real life by the architectural style of your own house or the size of your bank balance.

Perhaps the country house look is what we are all aiming for, whatever the period. Some years ago I enjoyed a – possibly apocryphal – story about the Queen Mother, who went to take tea with Sir Cecil Beaton and see his newly decorated house. Nervously, he awaited her verdict. 'How clever of you,' she said, 'to make it all so shabby.'

THE MAGNIFICENT DOLLS' HOUSE BASED ON UPPARK IN HAMPSHIRE WAS NEARING COMPLETION WHEN THE ACTUAL MANSION, IN THE CARE OF THE NATIONAL TRUST, WAS PARTIALLY GUTTED BY FIRE IN 1989.

PHOTO COURTESY OF MULVANY & ROGERS.

PART ONE

THE HOUSE

CHOOSING A DOLLS' HOUSE

Some dolls' houses are authentic replicas from a particular period down to the last detail of architrave or roof (*see* page 61). Others are imaginative flights of fancy, which may be roughly based on a real house, but with special features introduced at the whim of the maker or the prospective house owner (*see* pages 11 and 100). Today's craftspeople will make houses to commission incorporating anything the purchaser desires – limited only by his or her spending power.

You probably know already which period styles appeal to you – most people have a favourite. Georgian-style dolls' houses have led the field for several years now, echoing the current preoccupation with Georgian architecture. The clean, straight lines and elegant detailing of cornices, pediments and door casings always look good and scale down well to $^1/_{12}$ size. For the undecided, a visit to a miniature fair or a specialist dolls' house shop can be rewarding.

Often the dolls' house chooses you. The only reason for having one is because you want it; there is something about a certain house which appeals to you so much that you instantly begin making plans for how you would furnish and decorate it. It need not be new: you may still have the dolls' house from your childhood, one which has been relegated to the attic or played with by your own children until it has become overdue for restoration.

If the house is for a child, consider whether it is to be played with by more than one child, and their ages. A house designed with young children in mind is usually smaller and simpler than a collector's house, and sometimes has a two- or three-stage opening, like a magic box. For the slightly older child you cannot do better than a ready-made house from a range of strongly constructed houses with pleasant but not too detailed façades (which would add to the cost).

Think carefully about what you would enjoy most from a dolls' house. Do not rush to have it finished; much of the pleasure of the hobby lies in gradually finding the perfect furniture and perhaps making some of the contents yourself.

A GEORGIAN FARMHOUSE, TYPICAL OF MANY STILL OCCUPIED TODAY. THE WORKING SASH WINDOWS, THE DORMERS IN THE SLATE ROOF AND THE SIMPLE DOORCASE ARE SYMMETRICALLY ARRANGED TO GIVE A PERFECTLY PROPORTIONED FAÇADE.

A SMALL SCALE IS IDEAL FOR A FIRST HOUSE FOR A CHILD. THE LITTLE DOLL SITTING ON THE PARAPET IS ATTACHED BY A CORD TO A PEG WHICH HOLDS THE FRONT CLOSED. THE TINY INN, COMPLETE WITH SIGN, IS A MONEYBOX.

PHOTO COURTESY OF
THE DOLLS' HOUSE EMPORIUM.

DIFFERENT TYPES OF HOUSES

Once you have settled on the period for your dolls' house, you will need to think about its size, which will affect the price. The cost of decorating and furnishing goes up with the number of rooms, so you might not be able to achieve the effect you want in too large a house; on the other hand, you might find you have underestimated your enthusiasm, and quickly outgrow a smaller one.

There is a fundamental difference in the structures of English and American dolls' houses. The American house has no back; the front façade is fixed, so you need to turn the house round to look inside (*see* page 102). British makers prefer to follow European tradition and arrange for the front to be opened, most commonly with two doors. This has the advantage that the house can be placed against a wall. If you decide on an American-style dolls' house but space for displaying it is limited, you can put it on a small turntable.

Where cost is no object, you may decide to commission a house. This has the advantage that you can choose any exterior you like: the house can be finished in a facsimile of brick (*see* page 128), or made in beautifully polished wood (*see* pages 71 and 114). If you want lighting points in every room, this too can be arranged. You may ask for distinctive features – a belltower on the roof or a galleried living room – or you can have a scaled-down and simplified version of your own home. It will be finished to whatever stage you agree, so you can do as much or as little of the internal decoration as you wish.

However, such special dolls' houses are for the minority, and most of us will find something 'off the peg' that will delight us. Craftsman-made dolls' houses are often supplied in bare wood, leaving the purchaser to decorate and finish according to his or her own taste. A Tudor house can be a large mansion or a small cottage; Victorian includes the Gothic villa as well as the one-up, one-down artisan's dwelling. You may hanker after a country cottage, a Regency town house, or even a Palladian folly (*see* page 17).

For the keen carpenter, plans to construct your own dolls' house are available from a number of makers and dolls' house shops, and there are several books on the subject (*see* page 161). For the less skilled, houses are produced in kit form at a saving on the finished price (*see* page 162 for suppliers). Whatever you want, you will be able to find it.

PHOTO COURTESY OF MULVANY & ROGERS.

HOUSES MADE TO COMMISSION SOMETIMES INCORPORATE STRIKING FEATURES SEEN ON REAL PROPERTIES. THIS LARGE HOUSE BY MULVANY & ROGERS IS MAINLY GEORGIAN; THE COPPER-DOMED BELLTOWER AND VENETIAN WINDOW WERE COPIED FROM AN OXFORDSHIRE RECTORY, AND THE DISTINCTIVE AND HIGHLY DETAILED PORCH AND THE DOORWAY, WITH ITS CURVED PEDIMENT SUPPORTED BY CORINTHIAN COLUMNS, WERE TAKEN FROM RAINHAM HALL IN ESSEX. THE LEAD DRAINPIPES AND HOPPERS, STONE QUOINING AND VARIEGATED BRICKWORK LAID OUT IN FLEMISH BOND ARE REPLICAS OF THOSE ON A WILLIAM AND MARY HOUSE, A LITTLE EARLIER THAN THE GEORGIAN PERIOD. THIS DREAM HOUSE IS DOUBLE DEPTH, TO INCORPORATE A HIGH DRAWING ROOM AND ELEGANT HALLWAY WITH CARVED MAHOGANY STAIRCASE AND MARBLE FLOOR, PLUS 13 SMALLER ROOMS.

THE PRINCIPLES OF SCALE

Eighteenth-century dolls' houses were much larger in scale than those made today. Antique 'baby houses' were made for people who lived in large houses themselves, so there was no problem in finding space for a model house of any size. The Nostell Priory baby house is more than 6ft (1.83m) in height, while that at Uppark is 4ft 9in (1.44m) without its stand. In addition, the wealthy owners could include amongst the furnishings small bibelots and trinkets not specifically made for the miniature home. Ivory and silver miniatures intended as mantelpiece ornaments are used in many historic baby houses, even though not to exact scale.

THIS $\frac{1}{16}$-SCALE LATE EIGHTEENTH-CENTURY HOUSE HAS THREE FLOORS AND A TWO-STAGE OPENING, WITH THE STAIRCASE AT THE SIDE TO MAXIMIZE THE AVAILABLE ROOM SPACE. THE VERY PRETTY DECORATIONS WOULD BE SURE TO APPEAL TO A CHILD OR A COLLECTOR.

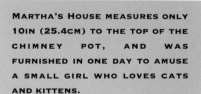

MARTHA'S HOUSE MEASURES ONLY 10IN (25.4CM) TO THE TOP OF THE CHIMNEY POT, AND WAS FURNISHED IN ONE DAY TO AMUSE A SMALL GIRL WHO LOVES CATS AND KITTENS.

During the nineteenth century, dolls' houses, now destined for the nursery, became smaller to suit the size of the average home and also to be convenient for a child to play with. Most Victorian dolls' houses still had discrepancies in scale, as at this time no one had given much thought to the relative sizes of rooms, furniture and dolls. Even allowing for the fact that ceilings in the Victorian house were higher than nowadays, many dolls' house rooms were disproportionally tall, giving them an odd appearance.

Today the internationally recognized scale for dolls' houses and miniatures is $\frac{1}{12}$: 1in is equivalent to 1ft (1cm represents 12cm). This is small enough to be defined as miniature, yet not too small for all the details of decoration and furniture to be seen clearly. The dolls' house itself is a sensible size, with room heights of 8in–12in (20cm–30cm), depending on the period.

Other scales are used, although they may not be universally acknowledged. Commercially made dolls' houses in the twentieth century were, until recently, made in $\frac{1}{16}$ scale. (*See* page 103 for another example of a $\frac{1}{16}$-scale dolls' house.)

Today's makers of miniature furniture stick mainly to $\frac{1}{12}$, but some craftspeople are willing to make in $\frac{1}{16}$ as well. In any case, many items of real furniture are made in a range of sizes, and a maker may choose to miniaturize, for example, a large chair or a small chair. If you have an old dolls' house you can still search out suitable furniture, although it may take a little perseverance.

A $\frac{1}{24}$-SCALE HOUSE ENVISAGED BY THE DESIGNER AS A 'MOUSE HOUSE' FOR A SMALL CHILD. THE DETAILED FAÇADE WILL ALSO APPEAL TO THE COLLECTOR.

THE GROUND FLOOR IS FITTED UP AS AN ENGLISH TEA ROOM. THE HEYDAY OF THE TEA ROOM WAS THE 1930S, AND FOR THIS EXAMPLE PERIOD FURNITURE WAS SPECIALLY MADE IN $\frac{1}{24}$ SCALE BY MALCOLM SEYMOUR-HOWELL. SCONES, CAKE AND JAM ARE PROVIDED; THE TRADITIONAL BROWN TEAPOT ON THE SHELVES, COMMISSIONED FROM POTTER CAROL LODDER, IS PROBABLY THE SMALLEST HAND-THROWN TEAPOT EVER MADE.

Another scale that appeals to those intrigued by minuteness of size is $\frac{1}{24}$. This has been pioneered in America (where even $\frac{1}{48}$ is now being made – *see* page 102), but is bound to remain a minority interest. The difficulties for the maker – of keeping to high standards while fashioning an object with details that can barely be seen with the naked eye – are formidable. It also presents problems in finding enough of the accessories – the paraphernalia which makes a house come alive and become a microcosm of real life. A $\frac{1}{24}$-scale house is an attractive option, but may remain with partly furnished rooms and no inhabitants.

INTERNAL STRUCTURES

Two-room houses can be very attractive, and it is amazing how much you can get into such a tiny dolls' house before it looks overcrowded. Four to six rooms, however, is more usual, and a dolls' house mansion would have nine or more rooms. The very largest are two rooms deep with extra openings at the back or sides, but such a house will need to be placed where it is accessible all round.

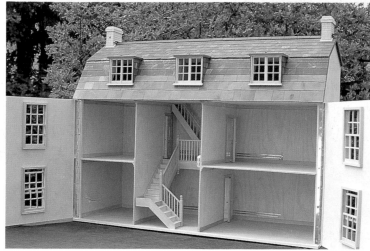

PHOTO COURTESY OF
GORDON ROSSITER.

THIS GEORGIAN FARMHOUSE HAS A FOUR-ROOM INTERIOR WITH THE STAIRCASE PLACED SLIGHTLY OFF-CENTRE TO CREATE TWO LARGER AND TWO SMALLER ROOMS. THE HOUSE HAS INTERNAL DOORS AND A DOGLEG STAIRCASE WITH FINELY TURNED BALUSTERS AND NEWEL POST.

Make the most of the space available: sometimes there is an extra attic floor with dormer windows in the roof space. If not, and if the roof hinges back, it is often possible to insert an extra floor to create more rooms or a loft. A dolls' house attic, like a real one, can be put to good use for storing small treasures which you want to keep but which do not blend in with your current decorative scheme (*see* page 91).

Chimney breasts are not essential – they can be external – but they help to dispel the box-like effect of a small square room. If they are not provided, you can put them in yourself when fitting the fireplaces (*see* page 135). The other interior arrangements depend a great deal on the placing of the stairs. A staircase is not a necessity in a dolls' house – after all, this is a fantasy world and the inhabitants can manage without one.

Stairs take up space, and in a very small house where the staircase is at the side of the main rooms, their presence can make it awkward to arrange the room settings to advantage. This is why a two-room house intended for a collector will have no staircase (*see* page 141), while one for a child will need the added realism of stairs.

In larger houses the staircase can become a striking feature, and it is most often placed in the centre of a house, leading up from the front door and hall as it would in a real house. Sometimes there are generous half-landings for doorways opening into the rooms on either side, or even a gallery running round at first-floor level. In a real house the tread of a typical step would be greater than its height, but in the restricted depth of the dolls' house the pitch has to be steeper in most cases.

PERIODS, COLOURS AND THEMES

As a dolls' house decorator, the first thing you have to do is plan the end result: what is your finished dolls' house going to look like? Unless you already have an exact picture in your mind's eye, take a long, hard look and think carefully.

Brick paper is never completely satisfactory for the exterior of a house, as it can be damaged too easily. If you are skilful you can simulate brick by careful painting, but it takes a lot of practice for someone without art training or specialist skills to achieve a realistic result; and, unlike a professional, you are going to be practising on what may be your only dolls' house. A smooth, painted finish in an attractive colour usually works better and is easier to achieve (see pages 49 and 84).

A lot depends on the degree of realism that you want, but in most cases a colour which would be suitable on a real house of the period will look good on your dolls' house. Colour-washed houses vary from region to region, but certain colours evoke distinct periods. A Regency villa might be sludge green or pale yellow. If your house is to be lived in by a retired sea captain it must be near the sea and might be pale blue, pink or white, like a fisherman's cottage. If you imagine it to be in Suffolk, then Suffolk pink would be the ideal choice.

You should avoid any sudden shock as the house is opened: try to plan a consistent theme without any jarring contrasts in adjoining rooms, just as you would in your own house. In every period people have had very definite ideas on colour schemes, and it is rewarding to do some research and find out what colours would be most authentic in your Georgian drawing room or Victorian parlour. The best way is to go and look at a restored property or room settings

in a museum; if that is not possible, do some reading – interior decoration magazines and illustrated books can be very helpful (*see* page 160).

When you have found a scheme you like, you may need to tone down the colours to a more pastel shade in order to get as much light as possible into small rooms. A dull sage green which looks perfect in a full-size Georgian house might be better in a paler, fresher shade of green in a dolls' house. Deep red carpet will overpower everything else in a miniature room, and a dark brown carpet will make it gloomy. In general it is better to use white paintwork for doors and window frames; however, gold used cautiously will add sparkle to a grand interior.

THE COMFORTABLE CLUTTER OF THIS VICTORIAN KITCHEN ILLUSTRATES THAT IT WOULD BE DIFFICULT TO OVERFURNISH A KITCHEN OF THIS PERIOD. CONTENTS INCLUDE A COSY RANGE, A DRESSER DISPLAYING AN ENTIRE DINNER SERVICE, COPPER AND BRASS UTENSILS, A TABLE COVERED WITH EDIBLE-LOOKING FOOD, AND BASKETS OF VEGETABLES ON THE FLAGSTONED FLOOR. THE RAG RUG, WINDSOR CHAIR AND CAT ASLEEP IN ITS BASKET ADD HOMELY TOUCHES TO THE SCENE, WHILE THE KNIFE-CLEANING MACHINE IS A REMINDER OF THE HARD WORK TO BE DONE.

DECIDING ON A STYLE

For most enthusiasts the interest and enjoyment of a dolls' house lies in creating a miniature version of a lived-in home, rather than a formal display of furniture. In real life most homes are an eclectic mixture of styles based on the things we enjoy. Each separate room will reflect the character of the individual, whether bookish intellectual, trendy teenager or dog-loving countrywoman. It is only in the interior designer's world that everything follows through with absolute consistency.

PHOTO COURTESY OF ELLIE YANNAS.

ELLIE YANNAS CREATED HER PALLADIAN VILLA IN THE STYLE OF PALLADIO, BASING HER DESIGN ON DETAILS FROM SEVERAL VILLAS IN ITALY. THE GLOWING EFFECT OF THE OCHRE-PAINTED STONEWORK AND TERRACOTTA ROOF IS TYPICAL OF MANY TO BE SEEN AROUND FLORENCE. THE MODEL OPENS FROM THE FRONT, BUT THE CUPOLA MAY ALSO BE REMOVED TO LET IN EXTRA LIGHT SO THAT THE DETAILED INTERIOR CAN BE SEEN MORE CLEARLY. THE INSIDE OF THE DOME IS ALSO FINELY PAINTED.

FASCINATED BY THE RENAISSANCE TRADITION OF MURAL PAINTING, THE ARTIST CREATED AN INTERIOR WITH TROMPE L'OEIL EFFECTS – THE STATUES PAINTED IN NICHES SEEM THREE-DIMENSIONAL. THE FLOOR HAS A STUNNING DESIGN, AGAIN SIMULATED IN PAINT.

An element of surprise makes a room interesting – the piece of lace brought home from a foreign holiday as a souvenir; the snapshot among the family portraits; the lopsided pottery bowl which was a present and which is treasured because of the love and care that went into making it. Although your house will be from a particular period, this need not limit you to including furniture solely of that time. After all, people live in inherited houses and often own both antiques and up-to-date equipment.

The exterior of your house will dictate whether it is to be a town or country house, and this is bound to influence your choice of interior decoration. Your imagined inhabitants will help you to decide whether they are living in, say, Georgian splendour as it might have been in 1780, or whether they are a modern family who have made some changes to their 1860 house while keeping some of grandmother's treasured furniture.

In real life the things that turn a house into a much-loved home are accumulated gradually, and the complete dolls' house also evolves slowly to become a home that suggests a lifestyle rather than a lifeless series of room settings.

Part of the pleasure of the miniature world is that there is no limit to what you can do. If you are fascinated by the 'Golden Age' of the ancient Greeks, or are interested in Roman history, there is nothing to stop you recreating a lavishly decorated version of a temple or a villa. You can do some research into the building styles of the time and commission exactly what you want, and provided your dream house is not excessively large, you may be pleasantly surprised at the cost.

We all live in a fantasy world occasionally – think of the numbers who follow the adventures of the characters in TV soap operas. A house or a cottage decorated and furnished as you imagine the scene in a favourite book or play can be fun to arrange. Part of the fascination is searching out miniature versions of all the things mentioned in the original story, so that everything would be recognizable to the characters – or even to the author.

PLANNING THE ROOMS

Start with a plan: you will need to decide how each room will be used. What kinds would you enjoy furnishing and fitting out most? The number of rooms will usually be less than in a real house, so you will have to make decisions at the planning stage because you simply cannot fit everything in.

The period of your house will be the guide to what should or should not be included, but almost everything is optional – even a kitchen. A country house-style kitchen filled with pots, pans, food and utensils always looks delightful when miniaturized, but if your house is a tiny three-room Georgian or Regency town house you can dispense with a kitchen altogether and still be historically accurate. Many Georgian houses in towns such as Bath were built purely for the purpose of letting to upper-class tenants during the Season. All food was cooked elsewhere and sent in when needed; the truly fashionable seldom stayed in to eat. In such a house the rooms can be used solely for

entertaining or retiring.

With the exception of the Tudor house, a drawing room is essential; later it became the lounge, and today a sitting room. A separate dining room is not necessary if you are short of space. Do you want one or more bedrooms? In a Victorian house you might prefer to limit the number of bedrooms and have a nursery or playroom instead; the Edwardian house could have a study, and the country house a library. The 1920s house would have a room for the maid, and the 1930s house can at last have a bathroom. The lavatory is most often left out of the dolls' house when space is short, and yet most people find the inclusion

WITH THE EXCEPTION OF THE DRAWING ROOM, GEORGIAN HOUSES WERE SPARSELY FURNISHED. THIS NIGHT NURSERY AND PLAYROOM HAS A BARE WOODEN FLOOR; A SMALL TABLE AND TWO WOODEN BEDS ARE PAINTED A SUBTLE TURQUOISE GREEN. THERE ARE TWO HOODED CRADLES FOR THE BABIES, A SPLENDID ROCKING HORSE AND A VARIETY OF SMALL TOYS, INCLUDING A MINUSCULE VERSION OF THE CUP-AND-BALL GAME THAT WAS SO POPULAR AT THE TIME. (THIS ROOM AND THOSE ON PAGES 41, 44 AND 46 CAN BE SEEN AT THE SHIPLEY ART GALLERY, GATESHEAD, TYNE AND WEAR, WHERE THE DOLLS' HOUSE CAN BE SEEN BY PRIOR APPOINTMENT.

A DOLLS' HOUSE SEWING ROOM OFFERS ANYONE WHO ENJOYS FINE WORK AN OPPORTUNITY TO CREATE SOME STYLISH MINIATURE GARMENTS. THIS 1930s ROOM INCLUDES A DRESSMAKER'S DUMMY DRAPED WITH A ROBE AND HAT; THE IRON AND IRONING BOARD ARE READY FOR USE, AND OTHER CLOTHES HANG ON A WOODEN AIRER. TREADLE SEWING MACHINES WERE STILL IN USE AT THIS TIME, AS THEY WERE LONG-LASTING AND MORE MODERN MACHINES WERE EXPENSIVE. THE SMALL CARPET WORKED IN NEEDLEPOINT IS BASED ON A PATTERN POPULAR AT THE TIME.

of a miniature loo entertaining – especially if the chain can be pulled!

If your house is large enough you can use the smaller rooms to carry out unusual schemes – a butler's pantry, a sewing or laundry room, or even a dairy. Only you can decide how best to turn your creative ideas into reality, but there is little doubt that today's craftspeople will have anticipated your needs.

LIGHTING

There is another decision to be made before you start decorating: whether or not to install lighting. There are two views on this: the first is that if the house is decorated and furnished to represent a period before electric lighting was invented, it would not be in keeping to include such an anachronism. The other opinion is that electric lighting creates such magical effects in the miniature world that it is essential. One further consideration – and perhaps the one which will have most influence on your decision – is whether you feel competent to tackle the work.

If the house is being made to commission and you want lighting included it is best to ask the maker to do it for you, as all your requirements can be planned to go in at the construction stage. But for those with some experience of electrical work, installing lighting in a dolls' house will be relatively straightforward. Lighting kits are available from dolls' house and hobbies shops (*see* the lists of stockists and suppliers at the back of the book); these commercially made sets are reasonably inexpensive, include instructions and work on a 4.5-volt system, using a transformer or a supply of batteries. In the long run a transformer will be more economical; check that it complies with the national safety standards.

There are some possible snags with these systems: one is that most of the light fittings are a little oversize, and with some the bulbs are permanently fixed in. Check before you buy that you will be able to change the bulb with a suitable replacement when needed. Another problem is that the plugs and sockets provided are also overlarge compared with the usual $^1/_{12}$ scale. If you use $^3/_{16}$in (5mm) self-adhesive copper tape wiring, which is thin enough to be inconspicuous when the house has been wallpapered and the flooring laid, the neatest solution is to remove the plugs and sockets and solder the copper wire directly on to the copper tape.

If you have never tackled electrical work before and are still hesitant, but really would like lighting in your house, there are a number of specialists who supply simple, ready-wired lighting systems which can be adapted to suit various sizes of dolls' house without having to resort to a soldering iron (*see* lists of stockists and suppliers). You can also obtain from the suppliers a booklet which will explain exactly how to proceed, written in terms comprehensible to the inexperienced.

Whatever you decide, you will be able to find working or non-working light fittings for every period, whether the originals were for use with candles, gas or electricity.

IT IS EASY TO IMAGINE THE GUESTS ARRIVING FOR AN EVENING PARTY IN THIS ELEGANT TOWN HOUSE. THE LIGHTING ALSO BRINGS INTO RELIEF THE DETAIL OF THE IRONWORK BY JOHN WATKINS AND THE STAINED GLASS PANEL OVER THE FRONT DOOR.

DOLLS

Planning the living arrangements in a dolls' house is always easier if you think first about who will occupy it. Early baby houses and dolls' houses always included a 'family'; most people today find that dolls make their dolls' house into a home in the same way that it takes people to make a real home. The contents of the house will then reflect their imagined interests and hobbies.

Early Continental dolls' houses usually contained very realistic wax dolls beautifully costumed in silks and satins. The English baby houses were also well populated, with the interesting distinction that while the 'family' were expensive wax dolls, the servants were wooden-headed. They were all accurately dressed in replicas of the clothes appropriate to their station in life –

PHOTO COURTESY OF SUNDAY DOLLS.

THERE IS SOMETHING VERY APPEALING ABOUT CHILD DOLLS IN THE MINIATURE SCALE, ESPECIALLY WHEN THEY ARE AS REALISTIC AS THIS LITTLE FRENCH SCHOOLGIRL.

the grander inhabitants wore silks, satins, lace and powdered wigs; in the Uppark baby house there are liveried servants, while the carved wooden cook in the kitchen of the Nostell Park baby house is in shirtsleeves and the eighteenth-century equivalent of a chef's hat.

Today you can choose wooden-headed, moulded or porcelain dolls, all beautifully dressed in the correct fashions for each period, or you can make or dress your own. For a $1/12$-scale house the average height of a lady is a little over 5in (13cm), and a gentleman nearer 6in (15cm). Wooden-headed dolls now have flexible bodies so that they can be posed.

If you do not want to have dolls because you want to arrange your house purely as a display unit for a miniatures collection, you may still find it helpful to imagine some inhabitants while you consider what to put where. However exquisite the furniture, it needs to be placed for a purpose, as though for use, or your room settings – however beautiful – will have the static formality of a showroom.

PART TWO

ACHIEVING THE AUTHENTIC LOOK

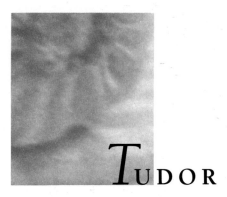

*T*UDOR

The Tudors left a unique architectural heritage: this was the first great age of domestic building in England, and that so many houses still survive is a tribute both to the care with which they were built and to the strength of their timber-framed construction.

Creating the complete Tudor environment in a dolls' house is a challenge. The majority of people at that time lived in one-room hovels with earth floors. However, most of us have a more romantic image of the age, based on our knowledge of Henry VIII and Elizabeth l, and will want to recreate a grander house showing the best furniture and interior design of the period. A $^1/_{12}$-scale Tudor house can give the same feeling of delight which we experience when we turn a corner in a country lane and see below us in a valley an ancient manor house, bathed in the golden glow of times past.

So how do you indicate in a house of few rooms the bustle and activity that went on to sustain the often perilous lifestyle of our forebears and their household of servants and hangers-on? The grand Tudor house was a world of its own: with no shops to rely on for provisions, the inhabitants had to make their own soap and candles, keep bees for honey, gather fruit to make preserves, hang their own meat and game to preserve it, and brew their own beer.

They kept sheep and spun and wove their own cloth, and grew and dried herbs to sweeten the atmosphere and give flavour to their cooking. The Tudors loved flowers, poetry, music and dancing, and found time for these pursuits too. Evidence of all these varied activities can be included in the room settings.

The popular image of the Tudor house is one of blackened oak beams and dark-panelled rooms, because this is what we often see today (*see* page 121). When the houses were built, however, the oak was new and pale , and in the rooms of the better-off the walls were covered with painted decorations and tapestries; the oak was often artificially darkened to follow a fashion in the nineteenth century.

The miniaturist who wants to recreate a Tudor environment needs to think back to what it might have been like in that age of ostentation and display. The Tudors did not value the antique – old houses were pulled down or left to decay alongside the great new houses built to show off the wealth and importance of their owners.

FAÇADE/CONSTRUCTION

A Tudor house is a showstopper. The craftsman-made Tudor dolls' house is built in much the same way as the real thing, with the construction of a timber frame, sometimes mounted on a stone or brick plinth, infilled with plaster. The beams supporting the upper floors extend to form an overhanging jetty which adds strength and allows the principal entertaining rooms to be larger than those below.

You can simplify this method to give an existing wooden dolls' house Tudor features, provided the basic shape is suitable. The trick is to study a real house or work from photographs, see how the main structural timbers are arranged and then draw a plan of how you want your finished house to look.

PHOTO COURTESY OF LAWRIE GREEN.

THIS ATTRACTIVE HOUSE IS BASED ON A STILL EXISTING TUDOR BUILDING IN HUNTINGDON, CAMBRIDGESHIRE, AND TYPIFIES THE SMALLER TUDOR HOUSE WITH JETTIED OVERHANG. PLANS ARE AVAILABLE FROM THE MAKER FOR THE REASONABLY SKILLED CARPENTER TO MAKE THE HOUSE FROM SCRATCH (SEE PAGE 162). LAWRIE GREEN BELIEVES STRONGLY IN INSTALLING LIGHTING, AND WILL ALSO SUPPLY A LIGHTING KIT TAILOR-MADE FOR THIS HOUSE.

A SELECTION OF MOULDINGS SUITABLE FOR USE IN THE TUDOR DOLLS' HOUSE. THE DENTILLED CORNICE BY BORCRAFT MINIATURES IS USEFUL FOR EDGING THE CANOPY ON A FOUR-POSTER BED AS WELL AS AT CEILING LEVEL IN A JACOBEAN HOUSE. THE PLAITED EFFECT WOOD STRIP CAME FROM A SELECTION AT A DIY SHOP AND IS IDEAL FOR SIMULATING THE CARVING ON THE FAÇADE OF A TUDOR HOUSE.

You can plaster over the wooden walls (*see* page 121) and glue on the timber framing afterwards, using $^1/_8$in (3mm) thick stripwood $^1/_2$in–$^5/_8$in (13mm–16mm) wide for the main framing, and $^1/_4$in–$^3/_8$in (6mm–10mm) wide for the bracing timbers. For realism it should not be cut uniformly straight; 'distress' it a little with a small hammer before staining with light or dark oak stain. A thicker piece of ornate moulding added at first floor level will give the illusion of a jetty.

In any period house, even though it may have been altered over the years, the windows provide a clue to when it was built. For a successful conversion from an existing dolls' house the windows will need mullions (upright divisions between each window section) and lattice panes. Another important feature is a solid-looking oak door with black iron door furniture and heavy strap hinges.

INTERIOR FEATURES

When converting a house to the Tudor style the structural beams must still appear to carry through to the inside, although there is no need to provide as many, as some beams might have been plastered over. Ceiling beams need to be fairly thick to appear strong; they are not there for decoration but to support the floor above. Square dowelling is suitable if you are putting in your own beams. They can also be made decorative: for example, glue thin strips of chequered veneer to the sides of the beams to reproduce a pattern of painted decoration popular at the time.

The wide, uneven floorboards of the authentic Tudor house are part of its charm, and it is worth putting in flooring which can be stained and polished, or left plain and light as it might have been originally. The scent of beeswax lingers in many Tudor rooms and would be equally attractive in miniature rooms, so it is worth occasionally polishing your floors.

Warmth in winter was of paramount importance, and you will need to provide large fireplaces in the main rooms: suitable wide ones are available in

LIKE THE REAL HARVARD HOUSE, PETER MATTINSON'S FINE MINIATURE VERSION BOASTS BEAUTIFUL OAK PANELLING, A WIDE FIREPLACE SURMOUNTED WITH PAINTED HERALDIC SHIELDS ON THE STONEWORK, AND IN THE PASSAGE THE HALF-TIMBERING IS LEFT EXPOSED.

PHOTO COURTESY OF PETER MATTINSON.

cast resin. Cast-iron firebacks, traditionally made in Sussex, were fashioned in elaborate designs, sometimes with the initials of the owner intertwined with other patterns. Miniature versions of these are made by Sussex Crafts.

A massive, elaborately carved wooden screen was a dominant feature of the hall in the larger Tudor house, with doorways through into the passage beyond. (Separate walled corridors were not part of the structural plan.) In the miniature room it is a simple matter to put in an oak screen near the back of your main room, and if you leave openings that are not filled with solid doors there will be a view through, with enough space beyond to include a table or bench. The screen need only be a couple of inches from the back wall; it is a useful visual trick in dolls' house interior design to lead the eye on to an imagined extra room.

THIS EFFECTIVE SCREEN WAS MADE FROM OAK VENEER GLUED ON TO THIN PLYWOOD AND CUT TO FIT THE ROOM FROM A CARD PATTERN. DOORWAYS HAVE BEEN LEFT OPEN TO GIVE A GLIMPSE OF PORTRAITS ON THE WALLS BEYOND. THE SCREEN IS FIXED ON TO BATTENS MADE FROM 2IN (51MM) WIDE STRIPS OF WOOD GLUED TO THE SIDE WALLS FROM FLOOR TO CEILING, PLUS ONE IN THE CENTRE, WHERE IT CANNOT BE SEEN FROM THE FRONT, TO GIVE ADDED STRENGTH.
THE READY-MADE FIREPLACE IN CAST RESIN IS WIDE ENOUGH TO ACCOMMODATE ANDIRONS (METAL SUPPORTS FOR BURNING LOGS, POPULARLY KNOWN AS FIREDOGS) AND A TRADITIONAL CAST-IRON FIREBACK. A LARGE BASKET OF LOGS IS A NECESSITY.

INTERIOR DECORATION

Interior decoration of the Tudor or Jacobean room was very different from that of later periods. Wallpapers had not been invented and floor carpets were non-existent: carpets were not for walking on, but were draped over tables to add richness and colour. Wooden panelling was incorporated into some rooms and carved to resemble folded linen, or painted with flowers, birds and beasts. Ceilings in the grander houses were elaborately carved and painted in bright colours.

Window curtains did not exist, but hangings and tapestries were used wherever possible to keep out draughts. Although the bed hangings in large Tudor houses now open to the public are often made of damask or brocade trimmed with gilt bullion cords and tassels, simple materials were used in most original Tudor homes. A coarse woven linen, sometimes with a red stripe, was a

THE 'PAINTED' WALL PANELLING AND HUNG TAPESTRY BRIGHTEN UP THE TUDOR ROOM AND MAKE AUTHENTIC DECORATIONS.

common covering for the 'second-best' bed (*see* page 34) – the one that was used regularly. The 'best' or 'state' bed in a grand house was a lavish affair kept for visitors.

Lighting was by taper or rushlight. If your dolls' house is wired for electricity use candle-shaped bulbs in black metal holders; the effect of appropriate lighting in a Tudor house can be magical.

Painted wall panelling is an attractive effect in a dolls' house, and can be achieved even if you have no skills as a painter. You need to collect small flower pictures from gift tags or greetings cards; these should be cut to a suitable size and glued to the wall, leaving a space between each one which will be covered by stripwood framing. A coat of varnish over these card pictures will give an antique-looking 'painted' finish as the varnish slightly yellows the card.

A tapestry can be worked in fine wool on size 18 or 22 canvas and then hung as a wall decoration. There are a few specialists who work on a size of 48 threads to 1in (25mm), producing museum-quality work which takes many months to complete.

ANTEROOM OR HALL

If there are enough rooms in your dolls' house you can include a small anteroom as well as the main parlour. The guiding principle of Tudor society was one-upmanship: visitors were ushered into a small room and kept waiting before being greeted and graciously allowed such hospitality as their host considered appropriate to their station in life. The anteroom might be panelled and would, if at all possible, have a collection of imposing family portraits to impress those kept waiting with the rank of their host's wealthy relations.

An anteroom is fun to arrange, as you can search out and frame as many suitable portraits as you can find. Good sources are the pages describing exhibitions and announcing forthcoming sales in interior decoration magazines, where portraits are clearly reproduced in full colour and are often of a suitable

PHOTO COURTESY OF IVAN TURNER.

AN ELIZABETHAN COURT CUPBOARD C. 1600. THIS FINE MINIATURE WAS MADE BY IVAN TURNER; EVERY DETAIL OF THE CARVING IS AN EXACT REPLICA OF THAT ON THE ORIGINAL PIECE. ON TOP OF THE CUPBOARD A SILVER-MOUNTED PORCELAIN TIGERWARE JUG IS THE COMBINED WORK OF POTTER MURIEL HOPWOOD AND SILVERSMITH KEN PALMER. THE SILVER GILT CUPS, GOBLET AND DISHES WERE MADE BY MARY OLNEY, AND ARE BASED ON ORIGINALS IN THE VICTORIA AND ALBERT MUSEUM COLLECTION IN LONDON.

A FINE DISPLAY OF PEWTER FOR THE WEALTHIER TUDOR HOUSEHOLD; POTTERY WAS A RARE LUXURY AT THIS TIME, AND THE POORER PEOPLE USED LEATHER DRINKING VESSELS.

size. Frames can be made from gold-painted $^1/_{12}$-scale mouldings; oval or round portraits can be suitably framed in inexpensive gilt frames intended for making jewellery.

Furnishing the Tudor dolls' house is simplified by the fact that people did not have much furniture. A table or cupboard with a display of pewter and perhaps an elaborately decorated chest would be all that is needed to complete your room setting. A simple bench would provide just the right sort of uncomfortable seating to make the visitor feel even more intimidated.

PARLOUR OR WITHDRAWING ROOM

The Tudor antecedent of our modern living room was the withdrawing room or parlour where the family could relax in private, away from the semi-public life which was unavoidable in a house with many servants – even a small manor house could not function without a large number of retainers, outnumbering the family by at least four to one.

Often the only chair was for the master of the house, and even his wife would have to make do with a stool like the rest of the family. But in time more comfortable seating appeared – the famous sofa still to be seen at Knole, Kent, was a great advance in style, and upholstered seating soon became popular – but was only affordable by the very rich. The choice of furnishings will depend on the status of our imagined inhabitants.

THIS PLEASANT PARLOUR CONTAINS A REPLICA OF THE KNOLE SOFA, MADE SPECIALLY FOR THIS ROOM BY JANE LONGDON-FULLER AND COVERED IN AN AGED-LOOKING GOLDEN VELVET. THE ROOM ALSO INCLUDES A SPICE CHEST WITH NINE DRAWERS, AND IN ONE CORNER IS A SMALL STEEL MIRROR, WHICH WOULD HAVE BEEN A RARE LUXURY. A BUNCH OF HERBS HANGS FROM A BEAM.

Another reminder of times past could be a spice chest. Spices were expensive commodities, kept under lock and key by the mistress of the house. They were essential in cooking to disguise the taste of stale or rancid ingredients, but would be kept safely in the parlour, to be doled out on request, rather than left in the kitchen.

Music was the main form of entertainment in the evenings, accompanied by singing and dancing if space permitted. Lutes and recorders were popular as even one performer could entertain the company, and in the smaller household the mistress of the house could keep her hands busy with spinning or lace-making while listening to the romantic love songs that were the equivalent of today's pop music.

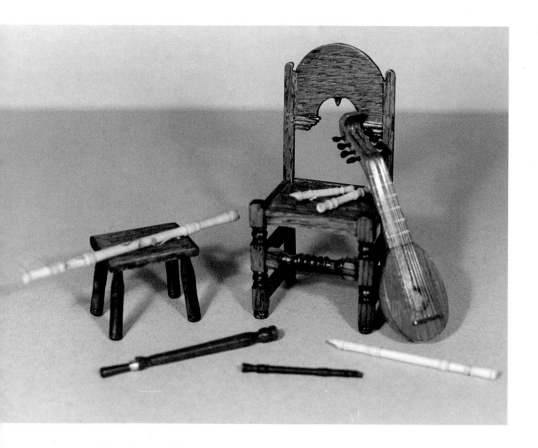

THIS BEAUTIFUL LUTE WAS MADE BY JAMES WHITEHEAD; THE RECORDERS OF DIFFERENT SIZES, ALL BASED ON AUTHENTIC ELIZABETHAN INSTRUMENTS, WERE MADE IN BOXWOOD AND EBONY BY WENTWAYS MINIATURES.

KITCHEN

The Tudor kitchen offers splendid opportunities to the miniaturist. The original was a busy place, especially in a large household where several scullions were needed to help with the cooking, all done in a huge inglenook fireplace. Big joints of meat could be cooked on the roasting spit, and cauldrons were suspended over the fire by means of a hook attached to an iron rod. A bread oven was set into the side of the chimney wall, and all sorts of ingenious iron attachments were used for hanging pots and pans. The kitchen gadget is not a new invention!

In the real Tudor house the floor might simply be of earth, but we can allow the inhabitants of our dolls' houses a little more comfort: ceramic

THE INGLENOOK FIREPLACE IN THIS WELL-USED KITCHEN IS LARGE ENOUGH TO ALLOW FOR A VARIETY OF CAULDRONS AND PANS TO BE HUNG FROM THE IRON ROD. AT THE SIDE IS AN UNUSUAL POT-CRANE ELABORATELY MADE IN THE SHAPE OF A PIG — IT WOULD PROBABLY NOT HAVE EXISTED IN TUDOR TIMES, BUT IS INCLUDED FOR PURE ENJOYMENT — BY TERRY MCALISTER, WHO ALSO MADE THE ROTATING SPIT, COMPLETE WITH ITS OWN DRIP TRAY AND BASTING UTENSILS. AS THERE ARE FEW RECORDS OF THE UTENSILS USED AT THE TIME I HAVE INCLUDED SOME INTERESTING LATER ONES. THE WOODEN BUTTER CHURN IN THE FOREGROUND CAN BE ROTATED.

AUTHENTIC TUDOR FOOD IS ESSENTIAL. THE VENISON PIE AND BOAR'S HEAD DRESSED FOR A FEAST WERE SUPPLIED BY WENTWAYS MINIATURES.

flagstones and bricks are made in dolls' house scale and can be fixed on with white fabric glue. You might want to 'dirty' them a little and strew some small bits of dried grass to simulate the rushes which were used to keep the floors clean; these were occasionally swept up, together with the accumulation of stale food droppings, and replaced with fresh rushes.

Dolls' house food is mouth-wateringly realistic, although for a grand banquet there were many special dishes which might not appeal to us today. You can lay out roast peacock, a boar's head with all the trimmings, or a blackbird pie on your refectory table.

Food was hung from the ceiling beams to be out of reach of vermin, and you may choose a ham or a brace of pheasants made by one of today's dolls' house food specialists, as well as providing a miniature bunch of sweet-smelling herbs yourself. For tableware use pewter plates and flagons; wooden platters were also in common use, and you can substitute flat wooden buttons of a suitable size with the centre holes covered by food.

BEDROOM

The most expensive piece of furniture in the original Tudor home was a massive four-poster bed. Constructed of oak, it was almost a small room in itself, as it had hangings that could be fully closed for warmth and privacy. If you decide on a craftsman-made bed it would be a pity to cover the bedposts and carved canopy; leave them to be admired. If you settle for a home-made bed it need not be a mini-masterpiece, as you can hide any defects with extravagant hangings.

In a grand house you could also include a truckle bed for a servant or a child; these were low enough to be pushed out of sight underneath the four-poster when not in use. Clothes and other belongings were stored in large chests, as wardrobes had not yet been thought of. In the absence of a separate nursery (a Victorian invention) you might include a cradle. The Tudor cradle was open, but during the seventeenth century the hooded cradle increased in popularity, especially in Scotland.

Bedding, like everything else in the Tudor age, was carefully graded according to rank. The main bed should have two mattresses: a thick one underneath, with a softer, thinner one on top for extra comfort. Sheets, if any, should be of coarse linen, and blankets were of rough weave compared to our modern blankets. The truckle bed should have only a thin mattress (these were usually straw-filled) and a coarse blanket – a piece of grey or stone-coloured tweed would be adequate in the dolls' house.

The best bedroom was as cheerful as possible, and the plaster walls were sometimes decorated with a painted mural of birds and flowers or a romanticized landscape with a castle or country house surrounded by fields and trees. Unicorns were popular when animals were included in the scene. Plaster provides a good surface for painting, and if your artistic skills are up to the task you would probably enjoy this form of interior decoration.

THE MASSIVE FOUR-POSTER BED TOOK UP MOST OF THE AVAILABLE SPACE IN THE NONE-TOO-LARGE BEDROOM. THE STRIPED LINEN HANGINGS ON THIS BED WERE DOCUMENTED IN AN INVENTORY OF BLAKESLEY HALL, THE HOME OF A WELL-TO-DO YEOMAN IN THE EARLY SEVENTEENTH CENTURY, AND HAVE BEEN TRIMMED WITH FURNISHING BRAID: RED, DARK GREEN AND GOLD ARE MOST SUITABLE FOR TUDOR FURNISHINGS. THE SMALL TRUCKLE BED AT THE FOOT HAS A ROUGH BLANKET OVER A THIN MATTRESS AND A WOVEN COVERLET.

GEORGIAN

The classical symmetry of Georgian architecture appeals to most of us. The perfect dolls' house is Georgian in its proportions: a square house with a central front door and an equal number of windows on either side – the basic arrangement used by the eighteenth-century builder, timeless in its appeal.

These houses have been an inspiration to dolls' house designers, who have made miniature versions of grand brick houses with mansard roofs and

PHOTO COURTESY OF MULVANY & ROGERS.

PHOTO COURTESY OF
GEOFFREY WONNACOTT.

THIS MINIATURE MASTERPIECE
WITH ITS ARRAY OF DOVETAILED
DRAWERS WAS COPIED FROM A
LADIES' WRITING DESK C.1720 BY
GEOFFREY WONNACOTT. THE
DECORATION IS IN TWO SHADES OF
GOLD, LIGHT BLUE AND BLACK ON
AN OLIVE-GREEN GROUND. THE
DOORS OPEN TO REVEAL A FITTED
RED AND GOLD INTERIOR. THE
GREEN LEATHER WRITING
SURFACE COMPLEMENTS THE
WRITING BOX, AND SEPARATE
INNER BOXES ARE FITTED INTO
COMPARTMENTS FOR PERFUMERY
AND PERSONAL EFFECTS.

THE BLUE STRIPED FABRIC IS A
PERFECT CHOICE FOR THIS SOFA
WITH REAL MARQUETRY INLAY
TRIM AND EIGHT LEGS; THE FRONT
FOUR LEGS ARE TURNED. THIS
SHERATON DESIGN SHOWS FINE
DETAIL; THE FRONT CORNER LEGS
LEAD UPWARD TO SUPPORT THE
UPHOLSTERY, WHICH IS
SEPARATED FROM THEM BUT ALSO
EDGED WITH INLAID WOOD. THE
DESIGN REQUIRED CONSIDERABLE
SKILL FROM MAKERS TETBURY
MINIATURES.

elegant curving staircases (*see* page 135), plain farmhouses with front doors topped by projecting canopies, and small two-storey cottages with bow windows and elegant fanlights (*see* page 103) – all stylistic variations of this period.

Furniture in the Georgian house was sparse by today's standards, but always well designed and made with care. Many miniaturists produce superb copies of the exquisite pieces still to be seen in museums and stately homes, and the dolls' house owner will have no difficulty in finding appropriate furniture.

The drawing rooms had a different feeling to the relaxed atmosphere of our present-day sitting room. It was an age of restraint, of rigid codes of behaviour, and this was reflected in the formal way in which furniture was displayed in the homes of the well-to-do. The miniaturist who decorates and furnishes in the accepted manner of the time can be reasonably certain that the result will be as attractive as the elegantly proportioned rooms to be seen today in the viewable houses of the period.

PHOTO COURTESY OF TETBURY MINIATURES.

FAÇADE/CONSTRUCTION

Georgian houses are instantly recognizable from their plain, well proportioned façades punctuated by a symmetrical arrangement of sash windows with panes divided by slender glazing bars. There is usually an elegant doorcase topped by a semicircular fanlight over the six-panelled front door.

The real Georgian house is likely to be of brick, often accentuated by stone quoining and keystones over the windows, or of stucco broken up by tall pilasters; exterior decoration is sometimes lightened by the addition of Adam-style motifs or plaster panels in imitation of a Grecian frieze.

PHOTO COURTESY OF HONEYCHURCH TOYS LTD.

A large Georgian dolls' house made to commission can be finished as brick, with an imposing portico and steps up to the front door, but for the purchaser of a Georgian dolls' house in plain wood it is a much simpler option to paint in imitation stucco and add mouldings to break up the plain front. Many late Georgian houses were faced in stucco which was scored to look like more expensive stone.

The pleasing two-storey Georgian farmhouse also translates well into the dolls' house scale, with the same regularity of window spacing, a chimney at either end and sometimes a dormer window or two in the roof. A plain, colour-washed stucco is usual, and a dolls' house in this style looks good in pale ochre.

The addition of slates adds realism to a plain wooden roof, and there are a variety of easy-to-fix slates from which the dolls' house decorator can choose (*see* page 131).

INTERIOR FEATURES

The Georgian house used a lot of wood. Wooden panelling was standard before wallpapers became easily available – in the eighteenth century the tax on wallpaper was so heavy that wood was the cheaper option. The fashion today is to strip painted panelling and leave bare wood, but most Georgian panelling was of pine, always considered an inferior wood as it is easily dented and scratched, and it was meant to be painted. There was a high skirting board, a dado (or 'chair') rail at the level where a chair back could accidentally be pushed against the wall – a purely practical measure to prevent unnecessary damage – and a cornice.

The wooden panels were outlined with mouldings and provided a ready-fitted extra frame for paintings. Internal shutters preceded curtains, and sometimes there was a window embrasure which could be used as a seat. These fittings make decorating the Georgian dolls' house straightforward but also mean that a mini-mitre block and saw are essential for cutting the wooden mouldings to fit correctly at the corners; this is simple with the right equipment (*see* pages 116 and 117).

In very large rooms in grand stone houses where the size precluded the use of panelling, the walls were likely to be colour-washed, and niches were provided to display classical statuary. Additional decoration was provided by plaster mouldings. If you want to reproduce a stately home the plaster work can be simulated by using small classical motifs in the shape of swags and

PHOTO COURTESY OF JOHN DAVENPORT.

PHOTO COURTESY OF MULVANY & ROGERS.

garlands, which are readily available from DIY stores and can be painted white and glued into place. In this style of room the doors were often of mahogany and the doorcases were picked out in gold.

The Georgian interior at its best is formal, elegant and sparsely furnished; well chosen miniatures can be displayed to advantage in the small size of the dolls' house room.

INTERIOR DECORATION

Window curtains were rare except in grand houses. Blinds were often used instead, in a variety of styles. A great advantage of fitting blinds in the dolls' house is that this gives a uniform appearance from the outside. It is easy to make a non-working blind (*see* page 153); one that actually pulls down is very difficult to achieve.

In the first half of the eighteenth century the availability of paint colours was limited – pearl grey, off-white, cream, brown and a whole range of olive-greens, including one known as 'drab', were used for walls. Sky blue was popular but had a tendency to fade to a greenish tint – in fact the familiar 'Georgian green' may have been blue to begin with. The convention was to continue the same colour over wainscotting and panelling alike, and also cover over the cornice to ceiling level. Today's interior decorators favour white cornices as well as ceilings, and in ¹/₁₂ scale the extra white gives the rooms a much lighter effect, if not a strictly authentic one. A miniature room painted entirely in drab green looks drab indeed.

Robert Adam introduced many new decorative elements in the Georgian period: he used blue, pink, 'Adam' green and sometimes deep red, with white paintwork and much gold decoration, in his stunning interiors (*see* page 43).

DRAWING ROOM

A Georgian drawing room should not be over-furnished – a few well-chosen pieces are all that is needed. Chippendale-inspired furniture looks at its best in this setting, and the 'Queen Anne' upholstered wing chair had also made its debut. The wings served the same purpose as the side panels on a Tudor settle – they kept out the draughts. One open fire, however magnificent its surround, did not warm the room very well.

PHOTO COURTESY OF HONEYCHURCH TOYS LTD.

These chairs were first seen during the reign of Queen Anne, but were made throughout the Georgian period. Much later there was a fashion in the 1930s for reproducing 'Queen Anne' furniture, and if all the pieces so described at that time had been made during her brief 12-year reign (1702–14), it would have been the busiest period of furniture making in history. These earlier furniture makers favoured walnut over mahogany, but the cabriole legs and other features remained fashionable for many years.

A firescreen to protect the ladies' complexions was always part of the drawing room furniture, usually with an embroidered panel as its centrepiece. One popular design was a pole screen: the oval or square panel could be moved up and down the pole and fixed with a screw fitting so that it was at a suitable height. Screens are available with removable centre panels so that you can embroider your own design. For those who do not enjoy needlework a good substitute is a piece cut from an embroidered handkerchief. Dip a white handkerchief into cold weak tea and allow it to dry to produce a suitable background shade.

Candles were the only form of lighting. They were expensive, and in order to make the most of the light a fitting with a mirrored backing to reflect more light into the room was designed. The amount of heat and smoke generated by the many candles required for a large function, not to mention the hot wax which sometimes dripped on to the guests, made the atmosphere

THE SILVER CANDELABRA WOULD HAVE BEEN MOVED TO THE DINING ROOM TABLE OR THE CARD TABLE TO ILLUMINATE WHATEVER ACTIVITY WAS GOING ON, LEAVING THE REST OF THE ROOM IN HALF-DARKNESS. THE BRASS-BANDED MAHOGANY WINE COOLER WITH TWO CARRYING HANDLES WAS MADE BY DENNIS JENVEY.

GEOFFREY WONNACOTT USED LEMONWOOD TO CONSTRUCT THIS DOUBLE-DOMED WRITING BUREAU, PROVIDING A SCALED REPRESENTATION OF PINE, THE TIMBER OF THE ORIGINAL PIECE. THE PANELLED DOORS AND WRITING FLAP HIDE MANY SHAPED DRAWERS, CUPBOARDS AND PIGEONHOLES. THE PAINTINGS OF BIRDS, FLOWERS AND ORIENTAL FIGURES ARE ON A RED GROUND. THIS EXQUISITE MINIATURE IS 6⁷/₈IN (17.5CM) HIGH.

PHOTO COURTESY OF GEOFFREY WONNACOTT.

distinctly uncomfortable. This was not a problem in the home: for economy, as many as four people would read or sew gathered around one candle to illuminate their work.

A card table and some musical instruments might also find places in the drawing room. Card playing was the most popular evening activity in social centres such as Bath, while in country districts the young ladies learned to play an instrument and sing, and were expected to show off their talent – or lack of it – to relatives and visitors. Admirers of Jane Austen will remember Mr Bennet's remark to his daughter Mary in *Pride and Prejudice*: 'That will do extremely well, child. You have delighted us long enough.'

LIBRARY

A library was considered a desirable status symbol by the Georgian gentleman of means and taste, and many fine collections were amassed at this time. If your dolls' house is large enough you would probably enjoy making a library and gradually collecting the books and specialized items felt to be appropriate for both study and convenience. A writing desk and equipment, a globe and even a telescope all had their place in the Georgian library.

For the mini-bibliophile, specialist publishers produce printed and bound books measuring no more than 1³/₈in (35mm) tall, with legible typeface, hand-coloured illustrations and tooled leather bindings. Such a book would be the centrepiece of any dolls' house library and could be supplemented by even smaller clothbound editions made specially for the doll-size reader.

To avoid bankruptcy, it is also advisable to copy the designers of original Georgian libraries and make some fake books to fill up the shelves. Robert Adam used rows of such simulated books (leather-tooled spines fixed to a wooden block) in his libraries at Kenwood and Mellerstain.

Several examples of desks and bureaux are included in this section, and this is particularly appropriate as the supreme test of the eighteenth-century cabinetmaker's skill was a writing desk or bureau. These fine pieces are fitted with numerous drawers, all dovetailed for a perfect fit and often with concealed 'secret' drawers and alcoves fitted with boxes for trinkets.

The outside decoration might be of lacquer, with tiny scenes of birds, animals and flowers picked out in gold or faced with marquetry, using hundreds of tiny pieces of natural woods to make a picture so smooth that it is

THE LIBRARY AT MELLERSTAIN IN SCOTLAND IS UNMISTAKABLY BY ROBERT ADAM, WITH ONE OF HIS FAVOURITE COLOUR SCHEMES BASED ON PASTEL BLUE, GREEN, PINK AND PLENTY OF WHITE. HE INCLUDED CLASSICAL FRIEZES, A PAINTED ROUNDEL IN THE ELABORATE PLASTERED CEILING, AND A TYPICAL CHIMNEYPIECE WITH A PAINTING INSET ABOVE. ALL THIS DETAIL IS COPIED IN 1/12 SCALE WITH BREATHTAKING EXACTITUDE BY MIKE POWELL.

A COLLECTOR'S ITEM: A HAND-TOOLED, LEATHERBOUND LIMITED EDITION. LILLIPUT PRESS PUBLISHED THIS MINIATURE BOOK ON DOLLS' HOUSES IN 1989. THE AUTHOR IS JEAN NISBETT, WITH ILLUSTRATIONS BY CAROLINE NISBETT. THE CLOTHBOUND EDITION FOR THE DOLLS' HOUSE COMES COMPLETE WITH DUSTJACKET.

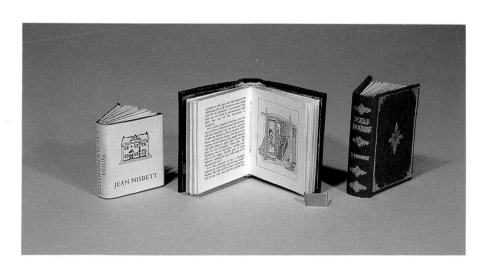

43

JOHN DAVENPORT INCLUDED 8 SECRET DRAWERS AND OVER 30 SMALL DRAWERS INSIDE THIS DUTCH BUREAU CABINET. THE DESIGNS OF THE EIGHTEENTH-CENTURY DUTCH CABINETMAKERS INFLUENCED FURNITURE STYLES IN GERMANY AND DENMARK, AND BUREAU CABINETS WERE POPULAR FOR A VERY LONG PERIOD, WITH THE DECORATION BECOMING MORE SOPHISTICATED.

THE ORIGINAL OF THIS CABINET ACTUALLY DATES FROM C.1880, BUT THE BASIC STYLE REMAINS THE SAME. HERE THE CHALLENGE TO THE MINIATURE CABINETMAKER WAS THE EXCEPTIONALLY COMPLEX DESIGN OF THE MARQUETRY INLAY. THE PIECE IS MADE IN WALNUT INLAID WITH A VARIETY OF WOODS AND STANDS 7IN (17.8CM) HIGH.

NO GENTLEMAN'S READING ROOM WAS COMPLETE WITHOUT A LIBRARY GLOBE. THIS ONE IS A COLLABORATION: THE MAP WAS HAND-PAINTED BY BECKY SAXE FALSTEIN, WHO INCLUDED SHIPS, WHALES AND OTHER PICTORIAL FEATURES FAVOURED BY EARLY MAP-MAKERS.

THE MAHOGANY DINING TABLE AND CHAIRS OF THIS PERIOD ARE HIGHLY PRIZED TODAY, AND EXQUISITE COPIES IN $\frac{1}{12}$ SCALE ARE MADE BY LEADING MINIATURISTS. THERE IS SOMETHING TOTALLY SATISFYING ABOUT THE LINE AND RESTRAINED DECORATION OF THESE PIECES. THIS FORMAL COUNTRY HOUSE DINING ROOM, C.1760, IS IMPECCABLY FURNISHED WITH THE ADDITION OF A SILVER URN, CANDELABRA AND WALL SCONCES.

almost impossible to believe it has been assembled in this way.

These extravagant cabinets are regarded as a special challenge by superlative craftspeople working in the miniature scale today, and each individual response displays their unique skills and imagination.

DINING ROOM

If your dolls' house has enough rooms you might like to include a separate dining room. Family portraits in gilded frames can look down on the mahogany dining table and Chippendale chairs, and a sideboard can hold anything you choose in the way of silver, glass, porcelain and food. A fine centrepiece of silver or glass would be placed on the dining table to hold syllabub or fruit, and silver candelabra were necessary at strategic intervals.

You might also include a wine cooler to contain tiny bottles of wine; small pieces of the crushed windscreen glass which often litters our roadsides make the perfect miniature version of crushed ice. And for total realism you should really put a pewter chamber pot behind a screen.

At a time when many gentlemen had returned from the Grand Tour with a vast quantity of artistic souvenirs from abroad, a marble pillar with a Greek statue or marble bust on top would not be out of place, and paintings of classical subjects were a recent addition to the family portraits. You do not need a great deal of furniture in the dining room; this allows you to concentrate on the frills. A table laid ready for dinner with a set of matching porcelain plates, glasses, decanters, tiny silver napkin rings and an ornate centrepiece is a recreation of a time when 'the rule of taste' was at its zenith and design was impeccable.

PHOTO COURTESY OF MALCOLM CHANDLER.

THE ARCHETYPAL 'QUEEN ANNE' CHAIR, BEAUTIFULLY MADE IN WALNUT WITH SHELL CARVING ON THE BACK RAIL, SHAPED SPLAT AND TURNED STRETCHERS. 'QUEEN ANNE' IS VIRTUALLY INTER-CHANGEABLE WITH 'GEORGIAN' WHEN DESCRIBING FURNITURE STYLES.

NO ONE HAS YET SURPASSED THE WORK OF THE LEADING EIGHTEENTH-CENTURY SILVERSMITHS, AND GORDON BLACKLOCK FOLLOWS IN THIS TRADITION IN THE MINIATURE SCALE. EACH PIECE IS HALLMARKED.

PHOTO COURTESY OF GORDON BLACKLOCK.

45

KITCHEN

Cooking a meal in the Georgian kitchen was still an achievement against the odds. Little real advance had been made on the Tudor cooking arrangements: the range had not yet been introduced, and the cook had to manage by using a variety of pots and pans suspended over a fire or on the solid hobs which were now built in on either side.

Coal was now commonly used as supplies of wood were running short, and this could be contained within a grate. The fireplace now boasted a mantelshelf above it to hold small ornaments or drinking mugs. There was a larger variety of iron cooking pans and kitchen utensils of wood or metal. Jacks operated by a series of chains and pulleys became more sophisticated and meant that one person did not have to devote most of their time to turning a spit.

THIS KITCHEN HAS THAT DELIGHTFUL, WELL-SCRUBBED APPEARANCE SO BELOVED OF THE NATIONAL TRUST WHEN THEY RESTORE A GEORGIAN HOUSE. THE REALITY WAS PROBABLY NOT QUITE SO IMMACULATE, BUT THERE IS NOTHING NICER THAN A WELL-PLANNED KITCHEN WITHOUT A SPECK OF DIRT OR GREASE. THE FLAGSTONES WERE PROVIDED BY TERRY CURRAN.

A kitchen of this period would have a flagstoned floor, and you can use miniature ceramic flags for this. But instead of being deliberately dirtied to produce a realistic effect as in the Tudor kitchen, they can be left spotlessly clean, allowing the variations in colour to show to good purpose.

The forerunner of the kitchen dresser, which originated in Wales, was a set of simple shelves often painted a dull green, which were used to hold crockery. Make your own shelves from stripwood to display a varied collection of pottery plates, jugs and white jelly moulds. All water still had to be brought in from a well, so Georgian kitchens lacked a sink; there was also no need for a store cupboard as food was stored outside the kitchen in a separate storeroom. But you can hang a ham from a hook fixed to the ceiling and put as much food as you like on a pine table in preparation for dinner.

BEDROOM

The Georgian bedroom is a lovely room to reproduce. The centrepiece is an elegant four-poster bed; unlike the massive Tudor bed, it is delicate, with slender turned posts and hung with chintz or simple white muslin. You can also enjoy yourself making festoon blinds (*see* page 153) and a draped dressing table; this delightful fashion has lingered on to the present day, and the bedrooms in many English stately homes contain a modern version.

THIS LOVELY BEDROOM HAS BEEN DECORATED IN THE FIRST STYLE OF ELEGANCE, USING EXPENSIVE WALLPAPER ABOVE THE DADO RAIL. THE FINE BED BY ESCUTCHEON LOOKS LIGHT AND AIRY, AND THE HANGINGS OF DELICATE MUSLIN AND LACE ADD TO ITS CHARM. THE BEDSPREAD IS HAND-CROCHETED.

PHOTO COURTESY OF GEOFFREY WONNACOTT.

THIS ELEGANT LITTLE BUREAU
WITH KINGWOOD AND TULIPWOOD
PARQUETRY STANDS ON CABRIOLE
LEGS. THE WRITING FLAP HIDES
MANY DRAWERS AND ALCOVES FOR
STATIONERY AND PERHAPS
JEWELLERY. THE SMALL SIZE OF
THE ORIGINAL WOULD MAKE IT
IDEAL FOR USE IN A LADIES'
BOUDOIR.

ANN DAVEY CHOSE A GEORGIAN
DESIGN FROM THE VICTORIA AND
ALBERT MUSEUM'S TEXTILE
COLLECTION FOR THIS FINE
COVERLET WORKED IN PURE SILK
THREAD ON SILK BACKED WITH
LINEN. FLOWER BASKETS AND
CORNUCOPIAS WERE POPULAR IN
BOTH EMBROIDERIES AND
PATCHWORK. THE SOFT GREENS
GIVE A PERIOD FEEL TO THE
COVERLET. THE STITCHES USED
INCLUDE SATIN STITCH, CHAIN
STITCH, FRENCH KNOTS AND A
TINY AMOUNT OF COUCHING
WHICH, ALTHOUGH NOT EXACTLY
THE SAME AS SOME OF THE
STITCHES WHICH WOULD HAVE
BEEN ORIGINALLY USED, PRODUCE
THE RIGHT EFFECT IN SUCH
SCALED-DOWN EMBROIDERY.

You can include a *petit-point* carpet and some little tables with as many 'trifles' as your pocket will allow or you care to make. A writing desk and chair would be useful; a wig stand, writing materials and some miniature paintings all add to the cheerful clutter. In my lady's bedroom there would be a small occasional table to hold the chocolate set made of fine bone china, and a workbox might fit in a corner.

The bedroom was more likely to be decorated with expensive wallpaper than other rooms. The wall up to the dado rail would certainly be painted, and in the dolls' house it might be better to choose off-white than any of the darker shades which were then in favour. Choose a small-patterned wallpaper in delicate colours or an embossed design to resemble the fashionable flocked wallpaper.

An alternative to wallpaper was to cover the walls with damask, and if you choose damask it should really be blue. Tax laws in the eighteenth century were just as iniquitous as they are today, and by some strange anomaly fabrics dyed blue were not taxed because the government wanted to encourage the flax industry. The result of this economical passion for blue wall coverings was a craze in France for English wallpapers, which resulted in many fine Gobelin tapestries being put into storage and being replaced by English flocked wallpapers – all coloured blue.

PHOTO COURTESY OF ANN DAVEY.

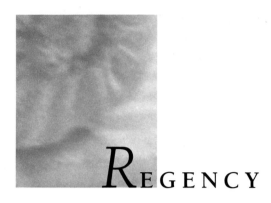

REGENCY

After the formality of the Georgian era came the less sedate Regency. The Prince Regent took the lead in both grandiose building schemes and fantastic interior decorations as houses and their furnishings and decorations became more frivolous.

THIS ELEGANT DOLLS' HOUSE IS BASED ON A REGENCY HOUSE IN CHELTENHAM, GLOUCESTERSHIRE, BUT THE DETAILS OF THE MINIATURE FAÇADE HAVE BEEN SIMPLIFIED. THE ROUND-HEADED WINDOW EMBRASURES WERE PROVIDED BY MANY REGENCY BUILDERS AND ALLOWED FOR DECORATION TO BE ADDED, OFTEN IN THE FORM OF A SCULPTED SHELL WHICH COULD BE COLOURED OR GILDED. WEDGWOOD-STYLE PLAQUES IN HIGH RELIEF SHOWING GRECIAN OR ROMAN FIGURES WERE ANOTHER FORM OF APPLIED DECORATION, AND THE SMALL REPLICAS ADDED TO THIS HOUSE ARE APPROPRIATE. THE SEMICIRCULAR PORTICO AND ARRANGEMENT OF COLUMNS WAS A STANDARD FEATURE. CARE HAS BEEN TAKEN TO MIX AN AUTHENTIC COLOUR FOR THE FRONT DOOR – A SOFT SLUDGE GREEN FAVOURED AROUND 1820.

The harmonious proportions of the Georgian houses were retained in the new stucco-clad houses that followed, but were lightened by the addition of elegant wrought iron balconies and curved porticos. There was such a housing boom at the time that many Regency houses were jerry-built, but this is not a problem with a dolls' house in this style.

The rooms of the fashionable were decorated with Chinese wallpapers, following the Prince Regent's example in the Brighton Pavilion. Chinoiserie became all the rage, and although even his contemporaries considered his Pavilion a little over the top, they nevertheless were influenced by the trend for Oriental decoration.

Regency furniture designers were inventive and enjoyed reproducing imaginative versions of Greek or Egyptian styles. At their restrained best the sabre-legged dining chairs and elegant sofas still appeal to us today, but some of the more way-out designs seen in Ackermann's *Repository* or Sheraton's pattern books were probably never made. Fitting out a Regency-style dolls' house allows full rein to our inventive capabilities. The interior will be both elegant and entertaining, with incomparable sparkle and style.

THOMAS HOPE AND GEORGE SMITH WERE LEADING DESIGNERS OF THE NEW CLASSICAL-STYLE FURNITURE IN THE EARLY 1800S. THIS SPLENDID DAY BED IS IN THE STYLE OF THE EBONISED AND GILDED PIECES WHICH FOUND FAVOUR WITH THEIR RICHER CLIENTS. THIS STRIKING MINIATURE HAS A NAUTICAL AIR WITH ITS DOLPHIN FEET AND SHELL-SHAPED HEADBOARD; THE FEET OF BOTH SOFAS AND ARMCHAIRS WERE MORE COMMONLY MADE IN IMITATION OF ANIMAL HOOVES OR LION'S PAWS.

The Gothick style initiated by Horace Walpole and taken up by the eccentric William Beckford was followed by all the trendy Regency decorators. It translates well into dolls' house size, being pretty and, above all, light-hearted. The fashion spread rapidly and many ancient houses were Gothicized with the addition of elaborate plaster ceilings and charming arched windows, which conveyed the new/old ideas without too much structural alteration to the family home. A plain dolls' house can be given early nineteenth-century Gothick features by very simple means, to adapt it in much the same way.

You can create a 'plaster' ceiling by gluing on a frilly paper doily or a combination of pieces cut from one over the first coat of white emulsion. Paint the second coat over doily and ceiling together. To represent the equally frilly plaster cornice, choose light and delicate white lace edgings and glue them in place. There is plenty of choice, and although it does not look like real plaster the effect is lovely, echoing the 'picturesque' feeling which is, after all, what led the Regency enthusiast to take up the style in the first place.

The pretty, frivolous style of the Regency developed into the more solid and sombre Gothic favoured by the Victorians and continued into the late nineteenth century, when William Morris and his friends preferred colourful painted and stencilled decoration, reflecting their passion for the mediaeval, to the wedding-cake effect of ornate white plaster.

FAÇADE/CONSTRUCTION

The Regency architect and his patron had eclectic tastes. Classicism enjoyed a tremendous vogue: stimulated by a growing interest in antiquities and what was thought of as a golden age of culture, many large houses were based on ancient Greek architecture. In dramatic contrast, the study of the picturesque encouraged the building of romantic fake castles, often with Gothick details. On a smaller scale, the *cottage ornée* was a popular rural retreat.

The Regency house which had the longest-lasting influence on the British way of life was the villa. Pioneered by Robert Taylor and James Paine, it was taken up with enthusiasm by John Nash and Decimus Burton, who built some of the charming villas in London's Regent's Park. The keynote of these designs was informality: they are instantly engaging, with their semicircular porches and sometimes a small domed turret. An air of frivolity crept in with the addition of delicately worked wrought iron balconies topped by canopies in

PHOTO COURTESY OF KEITH THORNE.

PHOTO COURTESY OF JOHN WATKINS.

THIS BEGUILING LITTLE COTTAGE ORNÉE IS BASED ON ONE IN FINCHINGFIELD, ESSEX, WHICH WAS BUILT IN 1800. IT FEATURES AN UNUSUAL CENTRAL CHIMNEY AND FIREPLACE IN WHICH MAKER KEITH THORNE HAS FITTED A FLICKERING FIRE. THE FRILLY DETAIL OF THE PORCH AND THE LATTICED GOTHICK WINDOWS ADD TO ITS CHARM.

FINE IRONWORK BALCONIES ADDED DISTINCTION TO MANY REGENCY TERRACED HOUSES. THE BEAUTIFUL CURVING CANOPIES WERE BASED ON THE NINETEENTH-CENTURY METALWORKER'S IDEA OF ORIENTAL STYLE. THIS $^1/_{12}$-SCALE VERSION BY JOHN WATKINS WOULD COMPLEMENT A PLAIN STUCCO HOUSE; IT WOULD NEED TO BE MADE SPECIALLY TO FIT.

51

the Chinese style. Even roof ridging became frilly. Stucco walls were painted in green, pale yellow or apricot, and relief motifs in the form of classical friezes added charm and interest. Ionic columns, Doric porticos and Grecian urns all found favour.

A plain dolls' house front can be transformed by adding some of these features. A simple way to add an architectural frieze is to glue on a strip of wallpaper with an embossed Grecian key pattern and paint over it in the same colour as the walls.

PHOTO COURTESY OF MIKE POWELL.

A SUPERB EXAMPLE OF REGENCY GOTHICK DECORATION, BASED ON A ROOM IN SLANE CASTLE, COUNTY MEATH, IRELAND, DATING FROM 1820. THE ELABORATE PLASTERWORK OF THE CEILING, GOTHICK WINDOWS AND BOOKCASES AND THE ELEGANT FURNITURE TOOK MORE THAN FIVE MONTHS TO COMPLETE.

INTERIOR FEATURES

Regency decoration has two distinct styles. We may choose either the plain country house in which Jane Austen would have felt at home, or a very grand house indeed. In either, the wooden panelling which characterized the Georgian room was replaced by wallpaper; furniture was now grouped informally in the middle of the room instead of being ranged around the walls, and because there was no longer any need to protect the wall covering against marks made by chairs being pushed back, the dado rail disappeared.

All sorts of grandiose schemes were instigated in the homes of the fashionable. Ionic columns were often features of the inside as well as the outside of the house, and were placed strategically in the hall or drawing room to emphasize an entrance or a striking piece of furniture. Niches and marble pillars were installed to display pieces of classical sculpture brought back from the Grand Tour, which always included Greece and Italy. Pediments and urns sprouted above doorways and bookcases.

Following the ideas pioneered at Sezincote and later in the Brighton Pavilion, chinoiserie was rife and the Oriental style influenced both decoration and furniture design (*see* pages 55 and 57). In the Regency dolls' house you can include both Oriental – Chinese wallpaper, 'bamboo' furniture and lacquer cabinets – and classical, with its busts and gilded cornices. In the original houses these disparate styles could often be found in different rooms.

The grand Regency house will allow you to include some of the more eccentric furniture of the period. But if your tastes are simpler you can have a cool, elegant house with sprigged or striped wallpapers, white paintwork and plain mahogany furniture (*see* page 115). Either will make an interesting dolls' house showing a distinctive lifestyle.

INTERIOR DECORATION

There are many contemporary sketches in existence of lived-in Regency rooms for us to copy or adapt – although even the most skilled miniaturist might baulk at creating a tent room, a scheme that was carried out by a few brave Regency decorators. White, gold, green and lilac were favoured colours, and gilded mirrors added sparkle. Curtain treatments were elaborate and striking: draped pelmets, tassels, swags and curtain poles with gilded finials are all features which can be copied and enjoyed in miniature.

Satinwood and rosewood with much inlay were popular. The chaise longue, that singularly uncomfortable form of sofa, only made bearable by the addition of a tasselled bolster cushion, added an air of elegance to the Regency drawing room or boudoir. There was a positive mania among designers for the exotic: ebonized furniture ornamented with gilded animal masks and Sphinx heads and feet 'in the Egyptian style' was made by Thomas Hope and others. This craze started after information filtered back from the archaeologists who went to Egypt in the train of Napoleon's campaigns between 1798 and 1801. It

THESE EXTRAVAGANT ROOMS WERE DESIGNED FOR ENTERTAINING AND MIGHT HAVE BEEN DESCRIBED AT THE TIME AS 'IN THE FIRST STYLE OF ELEGANCE'. CORNICES AND DOOR FRAMES ARE GILDED, AND THE SPARKLE OF CRYSTAL CHANDELIERS ADDS TO THE GLAMOUR.
THE STAIRCASE IN THIS HOUSE IS ONLY 5IN (12.7CM) WIDE, BUT BY CAREFUL CHOICE OF WALLPAPER AND 'FURNISHINGS' HAS BEEN MADE TO LOOK MUCH LARGER AND BECOME AN ATTRACTIVE FEATURE OF THE HOUSE. GOOD USE HAS BEEN MADE OF THE HALF-LANDING AT MEZZANINE LEVEL WHERE THERE IS JUST ENOUGH ROOM FOR A 'MARBLE' PEDESTAL TO DISPLAY A CLASSICAL BUST. THE WALLPAPER IS IN THE CHINESE STYLE AND THE STAIR CARPET IS SILK FURNISHING BRAID.

caught the popular fancy, and the fashion reached its zenith about 1810.

We can take pleasure in the excesses of the Regency designer and enjoy ourselves creating a small-scale house which includes some of these fanciful styles. Fortunately, enough skilled miniaturists have been inspired by Regency designs to make copies of this unusual furniture for our delight.

A TYPICAL EMPIRE-STYLE SOFA FEATURES EBONIZED WOOD AND SABRE LEGS WITH SIMPLE BRASS CASTERS. THE STRIPED SILK COVERING IS IN THE SLIGHTLY ACID YELLOW MUCH FAVOURED AT THE TIME. ALTHOUGH STRIPED FABRICS WERE SOMETIMES USED, WHAT WE KNOW AS THE 'REGENCY STRIPE' ACTUALLY HAD ITS HEYDAY DURING THE REVIVAL PERIOD OF THE LATE 1920S AND EARLY 1930S.

PHOTO COURTESY OF TETBURY MINIATURES.

DRAWING ROOM

For the Regency lady, sewing was inescapable – think of all those miles of sheets to be hemmed and shirts to be made for brother or husband. This work might be undertaken in a separate morning room, but the grander lady who

had the services of a sewing woman might still expect to spend part of her day industriously engaged in fancy needlework; in either case the dolls' house needs a worktable or workbox in the drawing room.

A writing desk or small table was also essential at a time when all communication with the outside world meant writing a letter; in Regency novels the characters spend much of their time writing, receiving and answering notes. A spinet or square piano was also usually provided.

Tea was served in the drawing room in the evening after dinner, and your dolls' house might include yet another little table with a tea kettle and

THIS SMALL DRAWING ROOM IS AN OASIS OF CALM WHERE THE HOSTESS CAN PLAY ON HER SQUARE PIANO OR PUT HER FEET UP ON THE CHAISE LONGUE. DECORATED CHIMNEY BOARDS WERE SOMETIMES FIXED OVER THE FIREPLACE IN SUMMER, AND THIS IDEA IS FOLLOWED BY USING A PAINTED DESIGN COVERED WITH ACRYLIC TO PROTECT IT; THE DESIGN IS A MAGAZINE CUTTING. THE PETIT-POINT CARPET WAS WORKED FROM A CHART ON CANVAS AT 18 THREADS TO THE INCH, USING COLOURS THAT WOULD BLEND IN WITH THE OTHER DECORATIONS.

A WORKTABLE WAS A NECESSITY FOR THE REGENCY LADY. MAKERS COLIN AND YVONNE ROBERSON FOLLOW TRADITION WITH THIS DECORATIVE PIECE IN FAKE BAMBOO AND LACQUER. BEECH WAS FREQUENTLY PAINTED AS BAMBOO AND 'JAPANNED' TO SATISFY THE DEMAND FOR ORIENTAL-STYLE FURNITURE. THE FLOWER DESIGN IS HAND-PAINTED AND THE INTERIOR IS LINED WITH BUTTONED RED LEATHER.

EVERY DETAIL OF THE STRINGING IS CORRECT IN THIS SQUARE PIANO MADE BY JOHN OTWAY. THE LID FOLDS BACK IN TWO STAGES TO PROVIDE A REST FOR THE MUSIC. IT IS 2¹/₂IN (64MM) HIGH.

A TEA SERVICE IN THE CHINESE STYLE, HAND-PAINTED BY JUNE BUTLER ASTBURY ON METAL SHAPES WHICH REALLY DID ORIGINATE IN CHINA. IT IS ONLY POSSIBLE TO REPRODUCE SUCH ORNATE SHAPES IN ACCURATE SCALE BY USING METAL

A CHAISE LONGUE SHOWING THE INFLUENCE OF CLASSICAL DESIGNS ON REGENCY FURNITURE. BY 1820 PALE WOODS SUCH AS SATINWOOD AND MAPLE WERE BEGINNING TO REPLACE MAHOGANY AND ROSEWOOD IN POPULARITY. THESE MINIATURES BY DAVID BOOTH ARE MADE IN LILACWOOD, REFLECTING THIS TREND. A PATTERNED FABRIC SIMILAR TO THE COVERING USED HERE WAS ILLUSTRATED ON A COUCH IN A SERIES OF TWENTY-NINE DESIGNS OF MODERN COSTUME, PUBLISHED IN 1823.

china in Oriental design. The English tea ceremony had become almost as formal as the Japanese, although briefer. And in some houses no evening was complete without a game of cards: if there is room you might want to have a card table so that your dolls' house inhabitants can play until the early hours of the morning. Gambling was a passion amongst certain elements of Regency society, and fortunes were won and lost on the turn of a card. In more staid circles people were content with a game of chess or backgammon.

A popular decorative device was a collection of framed silhouettes hung in a carefully planned arrangement around the fireplace. Likenesses were taken of as many members of the family as possible, surrounded by those of as many close friends as would sit still long enough to be drawn. At a time when every well brought-up young lady was expected to learn to draw and when paper-cutting was a popular pastime, many amateurs became skilled. To simulate such a collection, frame small silhouettes from gift cards in the gilt backings (intended for earrings) which can be bought inexpensively from craft shops.

DINING ROOM

Evening parties with music were a common feature of Regency life, and at the less formal gatherings there would be a table laid with a buffet supper. Even so, the table setting would be as elaborate as possible, with arrangements of fruit, flowers, candelabra and glass to give extra sparkle. With a little practice it is easy to shape a variety of fruit from one of the modelling compounds, which can be hardened off in the oven to fix the shape permanently and then painted. If modelling is not one of your strong points, the miniature fruit can be bought perfect in every detail. Try to include some grapes, which were a luxury item at the time.

The buffet supper is a good idea in a small room for another reason: it eliminates the need for a set of dining chairs. However, if you can fit them in and your budget permits, you may prefer to have seating at your table. A set of sabre-legged chairs with seats covered in silk would be ideal around an oval table with pedestal legs.

I have no kitchen in my own Regency house, but concentrated on grand reception rooms. In Jane Austen's novels the servants were seldom

mentioned but were unseen adjuncts to civilized life, so in a house with only four rooms I decided to dispense with the service rooms.

If you have a large enough house and want to arrange a kitchen, it would be much the same as the Georgian version. Equipment did not change radically apart from one great step forward, the introduction of the closed range. Even this up-to-date invention would have taken a little while to be put into most houses, but for the dolls' house decorator it means that you can use one of the attractive miniature examples available.

BEDROOM

The bed is always the centrepiece of the bedroom, and Regency furniture makers made the most of the opportunity for display; their beds were designed with imagination and *joie de vivre*. The elegant four-poster had tall, slender columns topped by pineapple or palm-tree finials. The head- and footboards were sometimes of japanned ware or papier-mâché inlaid with mother-of-pearl or painted in imitation of bamboo, or with flowers or Oriental scenes.

For sufficient strength in the smaller scale the dolls' house equivalent of this type of bed is made in metal painted to imitate lacquer. On such delicate designs the hangings need to be kept light and airy, and white net and lace are more appropriate than a thicker fabric.

ARCHITECTURAL PRINTS OF CLASSICAL ELEVATIONS IN GILDED FRAMES PROVIDE A REMINDER THAT THE HOST HAS BEEN ON THE GRAND TOUR. MIRRORS WERE OFTEN USED IN PAIRS AND PLACED AT OPPOSITE ENDS OF THE ROOM TO GIVE SYMMETRY, BUT IT WAS ONLY POSSIBLE TO FIT ONE IN THIS SMALL ROOM; IT IS A REPLICA OF ONE OF A PAIR IN THE DRAWING ROOM OF No. 1 ROYAL CRESCENT, BATH.

THE CENTREPIECE OF THIS SUPPER TABLE IS A GREEN-TINTED GLASS EPERGNE MADE BY LEO PILLEY. THE DELICATE TWISTED GLASS STEMS HOLD CONE-SHAPED BASKET GLASSES FOR SYLLABUB. THE DESSERT STAND HOLDS A DECORATIVE ARRANGEMENT OF FRUIT.

A scattering of small personal articles – books, bonnets, a bead-worked reticule or a shawl – all add to the lived-in feeling of the bedroom, and you can again use plenty of silhouettes or framed cameos on the walls. The washing and toilet facilities were often concealed in a cupboard, so you can choose whether to have them on show or not.

The Regency house is the perfect setting for a Chinese bedroom; any self-respecting house of any size had one somewhere. The delicate hand-painted wallpapers were sometimes set into panels or, if there was enough wallpaper available, the whole wall could be papered. No two panels were ever exactly alike as the designs were painted freehand, so the entrancing scene continued right round the room.

Giftwrap paper is the miniaturist's Chinese wallpaper, although you must search out a delicate pastel design; those which are too strongly coloured or too regular in pattern will not look authentic. The Oriental look can be enhanced by the inclusion of porcelain ornaments and furniture made in imitation of bamboo.

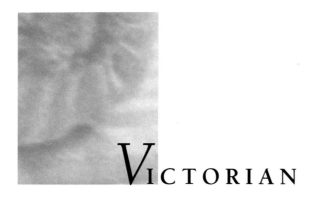

VICTORIAN

During Queen Victoria's 60-year reign the styles of houses and interior decoration and furniture changed dramatically. The Victorian home is often pictured as richly decorated, with plush upholstered seating, thick velvet curtains and over-furnished rooms filled with many little tables and whatnots covered with ornaments – and this is certainly what it became in the latter part of that long period.

PHOTO COURTESY OF PETER MATTINSON.

AN IMPRESSIVE DOLLS' HOUSE BY PETER MATTINSON, COPIED FROM AN EARLY VICTORIAN HOUSE IN GLASGOW. THERE IS LITTLE VARIATION FROM THE STANDARD GEORGIAN PLAN, BUT THE CRAFTSMAN'S REPRODUCTION OF THE LOCAL RED SANDSTONE GIVES IT A STRIKINGLY DIFFERENT APPEARANCE. THE ADDITION OF WROUGHT IRON RAILINGS AND STREET LAMP REINFORCE THE FEELING OF A TOWN RATHER THAN A COUNTRY LOCATION. THE WINDOWS AT THE SIDE ARE AN EFFECTIVE FEATURE.

ELABORATE GILDED OR HEAVY, DARK WOOD FRAMES WERE POPULAR FOR BOTH FIGURE AND LANDSCAPE PAINTINGS. THIS ORNATE FRAME, FROM AN INEXPENSIVE PACK BOUGHT IN A TOYSHOP, IS IDEAL. THE 'ANCESTRAL PORTRAIT' WAS TAKEN FROM A MAGAZINE.

Victoria came to the throne on the death of her uncle, William IV, whose short reign had little influence on interior decoration. The new Queen was young, vivacious and soon to be married to an artistic, talented Consort with an interest in architecture. In sharp contrast to its later development, the early Victorian house was light, airy and sparsely furnished. With the exception of very grand homes, floors were uncarpeted and shutters were often the only window covering apart from blinds, which were sometimes added to give shade from the sun or privacy to the inhabitants.

As the Victorian era reached the middle of its long span and the Queen became a remote, inaccessible figure who shut herself up with her grief at the early death of her beloved husband, Prince Albert, the Victorian interior became stuffy and claustrophobic too. This sounds depressing, but a mid-Victorian interior is tremendous fun to recreate in miniature, allowing us to use and display skills in needlework and fine sewing, and giving the collector the opportunity to fill the rooms with a splendid variety of ornaments and knick-knacks.

Pictures literally covered the walls in many Victorian homes, and it adds further interest to the well-filled rooms if we can search out suitable small paintings or prints to frame and hang. By reconstructing the intimate domestic surroundings we can arrive at a real feeling for the period on its own terms. The mid-Victorian room at its best was *cosy* – Queen Victoria's own word, much used in her journals to describe houses in which she felt happy.

The Victorian dolls' house comes in many guises, and the architectural style of the house itself will influence the decor and choice of contents.

FAÇADE/CONSTRUCTION

The streets of London today are still composed largely of terraces of houses which were built when Charles Dickens wrote his novels. A series of changes altered the appearance of the Victorian house from that of its Georgian predecessor. The stucco façades were painted stone colour to give an illusion of more expensive stone-built houses. Less pretentious houses of this period have the upper part from first-floor level left as brick without stucco cladding, but in dolls' house scale it looks more homogeneous to paint the entire exterior with eggshell finish paint.

Balconies at first-floor level and railings round the basement area were other features which carried on from the Regency style, but they became more substantial-looking: the fanciful extravagances of the Regency metalworker were replaced by solid middle-class railings which spelt 'Keep Out' to the poorer classes. The provision of a stairway down to a separate basement entrance for the servants and tradesmen reinforced this feeling of 'them and us'.

The elegant Georgian doorcase was replaced by a more grandiose entrance with steps up to the front door and a pillar on either side. The door was sheltered by the first-floor balcony, and light could filter into the long, narrow hall from a rectangular fanlight filled with stained glass. A rather virulent green, and later on black, was favoured for both railings and balcony.

Brass door furniture proliferated – a splendid array of doorknob, letter box, bell push and door knocker gave an air of importance to the black-painted Victorian front door, and all had to be polished daily by the servant because of the effect of the damp, foggy atmosphere on the gleaming brass.

Bay windows, porches, stonework balconies and elaborate cornices were later adaptations which blurred the initial simpler concept of the Victorian house during the building boom in the second half of the nineteenth century. But the Victorians loved their homes, and in dolls' house size these details become endearing rather than fussy.

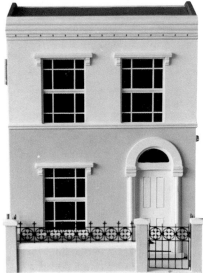

PHOTO COURTESY OF JOHN WATKINS.

THIS TWO-ROOM ARTISAN'S COTTAGE BY SID COOKE DOLLS' HOUSES IS TYPICAL OF MANY WHICH STILL LINE THE LONDON STREETS IN AREAS SUCH AS ISLINGTON AND PARTS OF SOUTH LONDON. IT DIFFERS ONLY SLIGHTLY FROM ITS GEORGIAN EQUIVALENT. THE RAILINGS (BY JOHN WATKINS) ARE A DELIGHTFUL ADDITION TO THE BASIC HOUSE.

JOHN WATKINS MODELLED THIS HOUSE ON AN END-OF-TERRACE HOUSE IN WALES, AND THE DETAILS OF THE FAÇADE ARE TYPICAL OF MANY BUILT IN LONDON AND ELSEWHERE BETWEEN 1830 AND 1860. THE ONLY VARIATION WAS PROVIDED BY THE DESIGN OF THE METALWORK BALCONY RAILINGS. THE TALL SASH WINDOWS ARE ALMOST THE FULL HEIGHT OF THE FIRST FLOOR ROOM AND ALLOW THE INHABITANTS TO STEP OUT ON TO THE NARROW BALCONY FOR AIR. IN THIS DOLLS' HOUSE A MINIATURE VERSION OF STAINED GLASS HAS BEEN PUT INTO THE FANLIGHT OVER THE FRONT DOOR. IN THE REAL HOUSE THERE WOULD ALSO BE A BASEMENT FLOOR, AND THE RAILINGS WERE NECESSARY TO STOP ANYONE FALLING INTO THE BASEMENT AREA AS WELL AS TO KEEP OUT INTRUDERS.

INTERIOR FEATURES

The Victorian town house interior was based on a standard plan. It was two rooms deep; the front door opened into a long, narrow hall and the staircase was at the side of the house, with a sharp bend or sometimes a small landing on each mezzanine floor. The first-floor reception room was L-shaped because of the arrangement of the staircase. It was usual to have double doors between the large and small sections of this room; these could be closed to make it cosier when company was not expected, and the smaller back section was often used as a dining room.

There was a large damp kitchen in the basement (no damp course was provided). In a four-storey house the servant's bedroom was on the top floor, ensuring that she had to go from the top to the bottom of the house to perform her duties.

A DOLLS' HOUSE WHICH IS REALLY AN ARCHITECTURAL MODEL. IT IS IN ¹/₁₆ SCALE, STANDS 33IN (83.8CM) HIGH AND HAS A LIFT-OFF SIDE INSTEAD OF THE USUAL FRONT OPENING. THIS VIEW SHOWS THE INTERIOR BEFORE FITTING ROOM DIVIDERS. AS THE FIRST STAGE OF ITS CONVERSION TO A DOLLS' HOUSE THE IMPRESSIVE STAIRCASE WAS ADDED, AND IN ORDER TO DISPLAY IT SATISFACTORILY IT HAS BEEN LEFT EXPOSED, NOT SHUT OFF INTO ITS OWN WALLED CORRIDOR AS IT WOULD BE IN THE REAL HOUSE.

THE VICTORIAN WASHSTAND WITH ITS TILED SPLASHBACK AND MARBLE SURFACE WAS EASY TO KEEP CLEAN. THIS PLEASING PIECE WAS MADE BY NIGEL LODDER, AND THE DECORATIVE EWER, BASIN AND CHAMBER POT BY CAROL LODDER.

PHOTO COURTESY OF CAROL LODDER.

This plan requires a certain amount of simplification in a dolls' house which is designed to be viewed from the front and is nearly always only one room deep. A lot depends on whether your Victorian dolls' house is large and spacious or whether it is based on an artisan's cottage or a small town house. Given enough rooms, any dolls' house enthusiast would enjoy creating a kitchen complete with range, ceramic sink, a battery of copper pans and some of the gadgets with which the inventive Victorians surrounded themselves. A bathroom is equally enjoyable, with a flower-decorated washbasin and lavatory, and perhaps a copper geyser.

But you may have to contain your ambitions. If your house has only two rooms you can still create an evocative interior, limiting yourself to a parlour, the epitome of Victorian gentility, and a bedroom with washing facilities included in the form of a marble-topped washstand and a hip bath.

INTERIOR PLANNING AND DECORATION OF THE 1/16-SCALE ARCHITECTURAL MODEL TAKEN A STAGE FURTHER. IN ORDER TO GIVE THE BEST POSSIBLE VIEW OF THE CONTENTS, THE INTERIOR HAS AN ALTERED VERSION OF THE NORMAL ARRANGEMENT OF ROOMS, WHILE INCLUDING MANY APPROPRIATE PERIOD FEATURES. BY CAREFUL PLANNING AND DIVISION INTO A FEW SPACIOUS ROOMS RATHER THAN MANY SMALLER ONES IT WAS POSSIBLE TO ARRANGE THE LAYOUT SO THAT 1/12-SCALE FURNITURE COULD BE USED WITHOUT LOOKING OUT OF PROPORTION.

INTERIOR DECORATION

Great attention was paid to detail in the Victorian home. The rooms were finished with plaster cornices and intricate ceiling roses. Skirting boards were higher than present-day ones and were finished with a series of curved grooves along the upper edge. Instead of the six raised and fielded panels of the Georgian door there were now four recessed panels surrounded by machine-made mouldings. Fireplaces were essential in all rooms and were made of marble or cast iron, lavishly ornamented with swags and garlands, and the grate itself had a tile surround of pictorial glazed tiles. The marble was not always what it seemed and was often only a painted imitation – this is a trick we can use to good effect in the dolls' house.

Patterned wallpapers were a feature of Victorian decoration. At first delicate floral designs were popular, but the introduction of aniline dyes resulted in the widespread use of stronger colours, and patterns became larger. In the dolls' house bold designs and colours need to be used with caution, as you want the effect to be discreetly charming rather than overwhelming. An adaptation of a Victorian design on a pastel background will give a more authentic impression than the same design on the original dark green or red.

There is a large choice of floor coverings for the Victorian house. Black and white floor tiles look good in an entrance hall, and the kitchen can have flagstones or pine planking. Fitted carpets replaced rugs, and the keen needleworker might enjoy working a dolls' house carpet in tent stitch, based on an original design.

Curtains were elaborately draped and trimmed with bobble braid or fringed. Thin silk is a good choice for miniature curtains, as the fine material can be draped and arranged correctly without any tendency to stick out. Never hem, as it adds bulk. Instead, run a cocktail stick dipped in white glue along the bottom edge; sew on trimmings by hand.

HALL

The entrance hall was important at a time when callers were always announced. A householder with a small income could afford at least one servant in an era when the average wage for a maid-of-all-work was £9 a year, so callers were received and relieved of their coats, hats and umbrellas before being shown into the parlour.

Even in the tiniest dolls' house you can give the impression of an entrance hall if you place an umbrella stand and a coat hook near the front door and hang a mirror on the wall. Where there is enough space you can have a hall stand which will incorporate all these features, and perhaps a side table as well. Victorian families were large, so you can add a number of umbrellas, walking sticks and hats to show that there is someone 'at home'.

Paintings hung on the walls of both hall and staircase will add to the period feeling. Animals and children were popular subjects: *Stag at Bay*, Landseer's most famous animal portrait, was reproduced and hung in countless Victorian homes; a sentimentalized portrait of a pretty little girl with a kitten or fluffy dog would be equally suitable. Animal heads with antlers were stuffed and mounted to be displayed on the walls, and miniature versions made of painted plastic are inexpensive and look surprisingly realistic.

Victorian entrance halls were full of warmth and colour. Floors were tiled in chequerboard patterns of black and white or red and white. You can also fit a stained glass panel over the front door, either one professionally made in acetate and metal strip or by making your own design on greaseproof paper: colour it in with felt-tip pens and glue carefully round the edges on to the inside of the glass or acetate fanlight provided. If your dolls' house is placed near a window the magical effect of the play of light on coloured glass will reproduce the reflections on to the hall floor.

THE FINISHED ENTRANCE HALL. LARGE MAHOGANY DOORS DIVIDED THE RECEPTION ROOMS OF THE VICTORIAN TOWN HOUSE INTO TWO PARTS. CEILINGS WERE VERY HIGH – 12FT (3.65M) IS NOT UNCOMMON – SO THE DOORS WERE IMPOSING. THESE 1/12-SCALE DOORS WERE MADE UP FROM KITS BY BORCRAFT MINIATURES.

THE SPACE UNDER THE STAIRS PROVIDES USEFUL STORAGE FOR SPORTING EQUIPMENT, AND THE CANE BATHCHAIR BY GWEN WHITE CAN BE KEPT THERE TOO. THE PAINTING OF THE ACTUAL DOLLS' HOUSE AT THE BOTTOM OF THE STAIRS IS A SMALL WORK OF ART BY WATERCOLOURIST KENNETH BIRD; HE HAS PAINTED THE HOUSE WITH ALL ITS TRUE ARCHITECTURAL DETAILS WITH GREAT SKILL, BUT STILL MAKES IT CLEAR THAT IT IS A DOLLS' HOUSE.

DRAWING ROOM OR PARLOUR

Creating a Victorian drawing room can be fun and gives an opportunity to include many of the pretty items which were popular. Remember that early in the nineteenth century the drawing room was relatively uncluttered, but as time went by more and more objects were added – occasional tables, framed photographs and paintings – until they overran the space available. So you need to decide on an approximate date and the degree of clutter you are going to provide as well as settling on the style of the contents.

Each chair had its own accessory, a hand-worked footstool sometimes ornamented with beadwork. The Victorian chaise longue was more solid than the Regency versions and was likely to be upholstered in velvet; the legs were also less graceful.

PHOTO COURTESY OF TETBURY MINIATURES.

THIS DRAWING ROOM HAS ALL THE COMFORTS NEEDED IN THE WAY OF FOOTSTOOLS AND A SOFA. A JARDINIÈRE IN THE CORNER HOLDS A LARGE ASPIDISTRA (EASILY MADE BY CUTTING TO SHAPE GREEN PLANT TIES INTENDED FOR THE GARDENER). A MINIATURE GLASS TERRARIUM HAS ALSO BEEN INCLUDED, REFLECTING THE VICTORIAN PASSION FOR TROPICAL PLANTS. THE HARP IS ACTUALLY A PENCIL SHARPENER PAINTED GOLD, AND IS INEXPENSIVE AND SURPRISINGLY SATISFACTORY.

THIS DELIGHTFULLY CURVY VICTORIAN SOFA IN THE GRAND MANNER WOULD LOOK IMPRESSIVE IN A DRAWING ROOM; A MATCHING FOOTSTOOL GIVES IT ADDED IMPORTANCE. RED WAS A POPULAR COLOUR IN THE LATE VICTORIAN INTERIOR, AND IN DOLLS' HOUSE-SIZE ROOMS IT CAN SWAMP EVERYTHING IF USED FOR THE CARPET. A SINGLE PIECE OF FURNITURE FEATURING THE COLOUR IS A BETTER CHOICE.

PHOTO COURTESY OF RUDEIGIN BEAG.

A FINE SELECTION OF NEEDLE-WORK; SOME WORK IN PROGRESS COULD BE LEFT TO SUGGEST THE VICTORIAN LADY'S EVENING OCCUPATION.

No room was complete without a workbox to keep idle hands busy. The Victorian lady might be employed in tatting; this is a little like crocheting, but has fallen out of favour as it is very time-consuming. Collars, cuffs and even tablecloths were tatted in intricate lacy patterns. Needlepoint was also a popular pastime, and could be enjoyed while someone else read aloud. The cliffhanging soap opera is not really new: the works of the leading novelists in the nineteenth century were published in instalments in magazines before being printed in book form.

Apart from reading, music was still the main entertainment in the evenings, when the strains of Mendelssohn wafted into the garden. Many families had a harp as well as a piano, and sheet music was kept neatly together in a canterbury. You can make dolls' house-size sheet music by photocopying real music and reducing it repeatedly until it is the right size.

KITCHEN

The Victorian kitchen had much more equipment than that of the Regency (see page 57). The coal-fired closed range gradually replaced the open range for cooking and was both more economical on fuel and not quite so hot for the cook. Running water from a tap over the ceramic sink meant that the servant did not have to go out to the pump for every bucket of water.

Today we can see many restored Victorian kitchens in National Trust properties in Britain and can select things we might like to include in a dolls' house. Copper pans and kettles and a dresser to hold a varied selection of crockery look especially attractive in a small size.

You will find it helpful to draw out a scale floor plan of your kitchen. In a room with only three sides and limited space the positioning of the range is crucial to the appearance of the finished room, as you need to set it into a recess or make a chimneypiece wide enough to take it comfortably.

Photo courtesy of Carol Lodder.

THIS KITCHEN IS FULL OF AIDS TO HOUSEWORK AND COOKING. COPPER PANS INCLUDE A FISH KETTLE FOR POACHING WHOLE FISH. THE PINE KITCHEN TABLE DISPLAYS AN ASSORTMENT OF CROCKERY, BASINS, A COLANDER AND JELLY MOULDS, AS WELL AS FOOD IN PREPARATION. THE CLOSED RANGE HAD AN OVEN FOR ROASTING, BUT MEAT ROASTED OVER THE OPEN FIRE WAS STILL THOUGHT TO TASTE BETTER THAN THAT COOKED IN THE NEW-FANGLED OVEN, SO SPRING-OPERATED ROASTING JACKS CONTINED IN USE THROUGHOUT THE NINETEENTH CENTURY; THE BOTTLE JACK (SO CALLED BECAUSE OF ITS SHAPE) WAS THE MOST POPULAR. THE EXTENDING BRASS TOASTING FORK WAS ANOTHER NECESSITY BEFORE THE INVENTION OF THE ELECTRIC TOASTER.

A DISPLAY OF FINE ANTIQUE PORCELAIN OR POTTERY ON A DRESSER WAS JUST AS POPULAR IN THE VICTORIAN HOME AS IT IS TODAY. THESE PIECES OF SEVENTEENTH- AND EIGHTEENTH-CENTURY DELFTWARE BY CAROL LODDER INCLUDE EIGHTEENTH-CENTURY FLOWER BRICKS, WHICH ARE THOUGHT TO HAVE BEEN USED FOR POTPOURRI OR LAVENDER. PUZZLE JUGS CONTINUED IN POPULARITY: THE SEVENTEENTH-CENTURY EXAMPLE ON THE DRESSER HAS A PIERCED NECK AND IS INSCRIBED, 'DRINK FROM ME, IF YOU WILL! TAKE CARE, DO NOT SPILL!' THE SHOES ARE LATE SEVENTEENTH-CENTURY; QUEEN VICTORIA HAD A COLLECTION OF PORCELAIN AND CAST HANDS, BUT SHOES MAKE MUCH PRETTIER ORNAMENTS.

The other problem is that both a range and a dresser show to best advantage from the front. The decision may be made for you if your dolls' house has chimneys, as it makes visual sense to carry the line of chimney breasts upward from one floor to another. (In the case of a corner fireplace in a bedroom we can assume an angle in the flues without stretching the imagination too far.) A piece of matt black card glued to the floor and extending about ½in (13mm) in front of the range will simulate a hearth. The rest of the kitchen flooring can be flagstones or pine floorboards.

Victorian kitchens usually had a cook, and the exciting dishes she provided are realistically reproduced by miniaturists who specialize in small-scale food to provide a tempting spread. 'Pretend food' has always been an essential ingredient in the dolls' house.

BEDROOM

A brass bedstead is a must, with the mattress covered by a patchwork quilt or a plain white counterpane, and you will need a marble-topped washstand (*see* page 62). Many makers provide these with simulated or even real marble tops, or you can create your own, either by painting the surface or by using a piece of marbled paper covered by a sheet of acetate: fix this to a plain wooden cupboard. A hip bath can also be featured if the bedroom is large enough.

THE ROMANTIC FEELING OF THIS BEDROOM IS ACCENTUATED BY THE CHOICE OF FLORAL WALLPAPER, LACE-EDGED WHITE BEDSPREAD AND THE NEEDLEWORK CARPET IN A FLORAL DESIGN. SENTIMENTAL PAINTINGS OF ANIMALS DECORATE THE WALLS.

Screens were popular, sometimes covered with green baize, to keep out draughts or for privacy. Fine examples of Victorian scrap screens survive in museums, and it is not difficult to make a small one for the dolls' house, but you need to plan ahead and look out for suitable pictures from greetings cards and in magazines.

The room comes alive with all the small items which can be left lying about – perhaps a fan or a shawl, a Bible on the bedside table, a dress laid out ready to be put on, and the Victorian lady's favourite accessory, a pug dog, complete with his own velvet cushion to sit on.

Papier-mâché furniture enjoyed tremendous popularity, and metal or wooden furniture painted in imitation is both pretty and appropriate. Tables, chairs and writing desks were made in this material, as well as firescreens, worktables and smaller items. It was light in weight and easily movable to catch the light.

PHOTO COURTESY OF CAROL BLACK MINIATURES.

THIS STRIKING PATCHWORK QUILT WAS HANDMADE BY CAROL BLACK USING MINUTE PIECES FROM OLD SILK TIES. AS SILK FRAYS VERY EASILY THE TURNINGS HAD TO BE AS LARGE AS THE SQUARES, COMPLETELY HIDING THE LINING, WHICH HAD TO BE TEASED OUT USING A LARGE DARNING NEEDLE. THE DESIGN IS KNOWN AS 'AROUND THE WORLD', AND WAS ALSO USED BY THE AMISH.

A CRAZE FOR COLLAGE RESULTED IN MANY FINE SCRAP SCREENS IN THE VICTORIAN HOUSE. THE SAME TECHNIQUE CAN BE USED TO COVER A METAL HIP BATH AND TURN AN INEXPENSIVE DOLLS' HOUSE ITEM INTO SOMETHING SPECIAL.

NURSERY

A special nursery for the children really came into being in the Victorian period, when children were supposed to be seen and not heard. It was usually ruled over by Nanny, and lessons were always taken at home by those too young to go to school. In many households children saw their parents for only a short time each day, when they were taken down at teatime for an hour's reading and talk with mother, and this custom continued in upper-class households until well into the twentieth century.

A Victorian nursery is a joy to the miniaturist as it is a toy collector's paradise, and many craftspeople make minute replicas of toys popular in Victorian times. The smallest are made of pewter, as it would be impossible to make such things as the animals for a Noah's Ark in such a small size in wood. A wooden rocking horse is perhaps the most exciting nursery companion, however, and can be made by a skilled craftsperson to resemble one in the original, as-new condition, or as it would have been after much riding by generations of children.

ALTHOUGH VICTORIAN CHILDREN WERE STRICTLY BROUGHT UP, THEY HAD THE MOST WONDERFUL PLAYTHINGS. ALL THE INVENTIVE SKILLS OF THE MAKERS WENT INTO PRODUCING MECHANICAL TOYS WHICH DID THINGS, AS WELL AS BEAUTIFUL DOLLS, DOLLS' HOUSES, THEATRES, FORTS, ROCKING HORSES AND WHAT WE NOW SEE AS HIGHLY DANGEROUS LEAD SOLDIERS. TOYS WERE UNASHAMEDLY SEXIST AND MADE SPECIFICALLY FOR EITHER BOYS OR GIRLS TO PLAY WITH, AND IF POSSIBLE THEY WERE ALSO EDUCATIONAL.

No Victorian nursery would be complete without a cuckoo clock; again and again they are mentioned in the children's fiction of the time, and the most memorable storybook of all, *The Cuckoo Clock* by Mrs Molesworth, has remained in my memory since I first read an old, battered copy in my school library. Cuckoo clocks seem magical to small children, and all dolls' houses need an element of fantasy.

Don't forget to put a fireguard round the nursery fire, perhaps with a few tiny garments hung over it to air, as was the common and unsafe practice. If your room is large enough you might also want a desk and chair, and perhaps a globe in a schoolroom corner for morning lessons. Life was not all play for the Victorian child.

PHOTOS COURTESY OF SAMUEL HALFPENNY (J. NEILL RICHARDSON).

LATE VICTORIAN

Unlike Regency villas, many of which were put up in a great hurry and flimsily built, the better Victorian houses were built to last. The jerry-built examples put up by speculative builders have long gone, but the nucleus of many British towns today is formed by the terraces of Victorian stock housing, which are as solid as when they were put up in the latter half of the nineteenth century.

THIS MAGNIFICENT VICTORIAN SCOTTISH BARONIAL MANSION IS 67IN (1M70) TALL, 53IN (1M34) WIDE AND 20IN (50.8CM) DEEP, AND HAS THREE FLOORS AND THE STAIRCASE IN A CENTRAL TOWER WHICH IS A FEATURE OF SCOTTISH HOUSES. MANY NOUVEAU-RICHE VICTORIANS BUILT THEMSELVES SUCH A HOUSE IN THE MIDDLE OF THE GROUSE MOORS IN SCOTLAND. ALLEMUIR HOUSE WAS MADE BY NEILL RICHARDSON IN OAK AND ELM, POLISHED WITH BEESWAX TO ENHANCE THE NATURAL BEAUTY OF THE WOOD. EVERY HOUSE BY THIS MAKER IS DESIGNED AND MADE WITH ITS OWN UNIQUE FEATURES.

PTARMIGAN LODGE WAS SPECIALLY MADE AS AN ADDITION TO THE ALLEMUIR ESTATE AS A GAMEKEEPER'S COTTAGE. THIS SOLID LITTLE HOUSE MEASURES 20IN (50.8CM) X 30IN (76.2CM); THE DETAILS OF PORCH AND BAY WINDOW ARE AUTHENTIC. IT RESEMBLES THE DOLLS' HOUSE MADE FOR MANY VICTORIAN CHILDREN, BUT IS IN BETTER QUALITY WOOD WITH A MUCH FINER FINISH, ALL CORRECTLY SCALED DOWN. THE GENUINE VICTORIAN DOLLS' HOUSE, ALTHOUGH ATMOSPHERIC AND ATTRACTIVE, WAS OFTEN MADE OF VERY THICK WOOD, SO THE WALLS BETWEEN ROOMS AND DOORS OR DOORWAYS WERE OUT OF SCALE.

PHOTO COURTESY OF SAMUEL HALFPENNY (J. NEILL RICHARDSON).

The Victorian dolls' house, like its prototype, adapts well to changing styles in decoration. Today's architects often live in Victorian houses which they decorate with pale walls, Bauhaus furniture and tall green plants. Modern paintings hang on the walls, there are blinds instead of curtains at the windows, and the floors are covered with cork tiles or pale fitted carpets. Kitchens are shiny white or dark green, and lighting is ultra-modern. It is an interesting experience to decorate and furnish a Victorian dolls' house as though it were lived in by a modern artistic family, and just as valid as sticking rigidly to period.

There is another style, too: the Victorian country house had its heyday when tycoons who had made fortunes in industry in the newly mechanized age wanted to move up in the social scale. In order to do this they needed a country estate, and as they had not inherited one they had to buy land and create their own. The sort of house they built makes a wonderful dolls' house. It has many rooms, but will inevitably be costly and built to commission rather than readily available.

The style is also classified as Scottish Baronial, and often has Gothic-inspired decoration. Turrets, towers and coats of arms sprouted everywhere; the late-Victorian country gentleman was banished to a smoking room specially provided for him in an airy tower, away from his wife's pretty boudoir.

MID–LATE VICTORIAN INTERIOR

Dolls' house furniture made in Taiwan faithfully mimics Victorian designs. It is inexpensive and can be useful in the period dolls' house, especially if supplemented with a few beautiful craftsman-made pieces. Upholstered furniture had at last arrived as the commonest form of seating in the parlour, and people were able to sit down comfortably and relax.

PHOTO COURTESY OF RUDEIGIN BEAG.

A BEAUTIFULLY MADE WASHSTAND FROM RUDEIGIN BEAG, WHICH ALTHOUGH BASED ON AN EARLIER CHIPPENDALE DESIGN WOULD STILL BE FOUND IN A VICTORIAN COUNTRY HOUSE BEDROOM. THE PIECE MIGHT HAVE BEEN RELEGATED TO THE MASTER'S DRESSING ROOM RATHER THAN THE MORE FEMININE BEDROOM. CHIPPENDALE'S WASHSTAND WAS VERY PRACTICAL: THERE IS A RAIL FOR A TOWEL AT ONE SIDE AND A NARROW SHELF FOR SOAP DISH, SHAVING EQUIPMENT ETC.

Wall-to-wall carpeting was another innovation – it was only later that the British took to leaving a surround of bare boards around a square of carpet. Victoria and Albert pioneered the use of tartan carpet at Balmoral, and this is easy to reproduce in the dolls' house; all you need is some fine woollen plaid material cut to size. Avoid tartans with a dark green or bright red background; one makes everything look dark, and the other dominates.

Modesty reigned in the parlour; everything that could be covered up, was. Tables were draped with heavy chenille tablecloths with fringed edgings. Mantelshelves were provided with an edging of braid-edged velvet, and chairs were given antimacassars (a rectangular covering laid over the chair back) made of the newly popular Nottingham lace, to protect them from the fashionable hair oil used by gentlemen. Even chair legs were sometimes discreetly draped.

As gas lighting became more common, daylight was no longer essential inside the house, and windows became festooned with layers of curtains to keep out the sun (which might fade the new furniture) and keep in the warmth provided by the coal fire.

PHOTO COURTESY OF RUDEIGIN BEAG.

AN EMBROIDERY STAND IN MAHOGANY WITH TURNED COLUMNS AND STRETCHERS WOULD MAKE A USEFUL ADDITION TO THE DRAWING ROOM, PARTICULARLY WITH SOME UNFINISHED WORK READY MOUNTED. THESE ARE MADE BY HUSBAND AND WIFE TEAM RUDEIGIN BEAG.

VICTORIAN GOLD-LEAF DECANTER AND VASE WITH ENCASED GOLD-LEAF DECORATION. ENGLISH FACTORY-MADE C.1870, WITH A STRONG VENETIAN INFLUENCE, MINIATURIZED BY EDWARD HILL.

While the gentlemen were out shooting, the Victorian lady was often busy with her needle. Berlin woolwork (tent stitch worked on canvas) was so popular that many households left a piece of work permanently set up in a frame in the drawing room so that anyone with time on their hands could sit down and fill in a small section. Practically everything could be covered in such canvas work – screens, cushions, pictures, chairs and footstools were all considered suitable for this treatment. So the late-Victorian house is a delight to someone who enjoys *petit-point* and can reproduce some of these items in miniature.

PHOTO COURTESY OF EDWARD HILL.

WILLIAM MORRIS

William Morris's imaginative designs for textiles and interior decoration led to a radical change in the way people perceived their home environment in the late nineteenth century. A man of ideas, writer, poet and in his later years political agitator, he was the most influential designer of his age and caused upheaval in the decorating world of his time.

His natural-looking fabrics and wallpapers and recommendations for white paintwork, uncarpeted wooden floors and handmade wall hangings came as a shock to a public used to dark red plush, heavy drapes at all the windows and the then popular cluttered look. Morris wanted the clean lines of more simple furniture to be on view, to have space and light, with just a few ornaments and beautiful paintings making a greater impact in sparsely furnished rooms.

He abhorred machine-made furniture and wanted to return to traditional methods where every piece was made by one craftsman from start to finish. He believed that everyone, rich or poor, deserved something beautiful to look at and that simple, well executed designs could be just as rewarding as ornate ones. Sadly, his ambitions could not be fully achieved because the costs of handmade work were too high for most people.

There is no shortage of reference material for those wishing to create a William Morris-style interior. More has been written about him in the past decade than any other designer; but words and pictures alone will not convey the tranquillity of a room decorated and furnished as Morris designed it. Go if you can to Kelmscott in Oxfordshire, to Standen in Sussex, or to Wightwick Manor in the West Midlands, all open to the public on certain days in the

THE HALL AND DRAWING ROOM ARE COMBINED TO PRODUCE USEFUL AREAS FOR A VARIETY OF ACTIVITIES, JUST AS MORRIS PREFERRED. THE SMALL TABLE AND CHAIR CAN BE USED FOR READING, WRITING OR TAKING REFRESHMENT. THE PAINTING OF JANEY MORRIS AS PROSERPINE WAS COPIED FROM A ROSSETTI PORTRAIT BY HELEN SCOTT-LANGLEY. THE LIBERTY FABRIC USED IN THE ART NOUVEAU SCREEN AT THE FOOT OF THE STAIRS CONTINUES THE DEVELOPMENT OF IDEAS.

THE BEDROOM FURNISHINGS INCLUDE AN EARLY TWENTIETH-CENTURY HEAL'S BED AND A WASHSTAND IN A DESIGN MUCH SIMPLER THAN THE FUSSY STYLES FAVOURED AT THE END OF THE NINETEENTH CENTURY. THE DRAWING OF MORRIS AND BURNE-JONES OVER THE BED WAS REDUCED BY PHOTOCOPYING A PRINT IN A BOOK.

summer months. The uncluttered beauty of these rooms, once seen, is difficult to forget.

Morris and his friends Burne-Jones and Rossetti began an artistic partnership when they met at Oxford, leading to the foundation of Morris and Company and also the beginning of the Arts and Crafts movement. This style became known to a wider public when Ambrose Heal, himself a designer of note, sold Arts and Crafts furniture and fabrics through his store in London. Simplified versions of the style eventually percolated through into the middle-class homes of the 1920s and 1930s.

It can be rewarding to follow this progression of ideas in a large dolls' house, and one bedroom in the house illustrated has been furnished with copies of Heal's furniture made early in the twentieth century.

FAÇADE/CONSTRUCTION

William Morris moved several times during his artistic career. His first married home, Red House in Kent, was built for him by his architect friend Philip Webb. It incorporated many of Morris's own ideas on how a house should be arranged.

THE EXTERIOR OF THE COTSWOLD DOLLS' HOUSE, AFFORDING NO CLUES TO THE WILLIAM MORRIS-STYLE INTERIOR.

The house which he came to love the most was Kelmscott in Oxfordshire, originally a substantial farmhouse built of Cotswold stone and described vividly in his *News from Nowhere*. The frontispiece of this, his most widely known and appreciated book (published in 1892 by his own Kelmscott Press), is a drawing of Kelmscott by C.M.Gere, with a typical Morris border of entwined acanthus leaves. The words underneath begin: 'This is the picture of the old house by the Thames to which the people of this story went' – who could resist basing a dolls' house on such an evocative idea?

To have an exact facsimile of Kelmscott would be too expensive for most of us. However, since the house was not built to Morris's own design and so is not crucial to his ideas, you can use a house in the vernacular style of the region. The one illustrated is a Cotswold-style house with the detailing seen on houses in this part of England – quoining, keystones over windows, deep windowsills and an elegant roof parapet, which are all made of stone in the originals.

The stone in the vicinity of Kelmscott, at the south-eastern corner of the Cotswolds, is greyish rather than the more golden stone further north. But there is no harm in a little artistic licence, so the colouring can be based on the richly glowing tones to be seen only in certain Cotswold villages where the iron content of the local stone is high enough to have turned it this amazing yellow-gold. A technique for achieving this finish is given on page 131.

INTERIOR DECORATION

Rooms in a Morris-style house are not dedicated to a particular use in the same way as Tudor, Georgian or Victorian rooms. The morning room, anteroom or music room do not feature here. Morris, a committed workaholic, liked the idea of being able to write or design wherever he happened to be. 'A drawing room ought to look as if some kind of work could be done in it less toilsome than being bored,' he wrote.

Even the kitchen need not be limited to a single function. Morris had an expansive personality – a convivial, jovial fellow to his friends, he was given to appearing from the cellar with several bottles of wine, ready for an evening of conversation, sometimes heated discussion and good cheer. He hated the Victorian idea of the formal parlour and was much more inclined to enjoy sitting on a high-backed settle in a flagstoned kitchen. No table in Morris's home was ever adorned with a cloth, as he felt that the beauty of the wood and joinery should be seen.

In Morris rooms the paintwork was always white, with the colour and decoration provided by fabrics, wall hangings, tiles and occasionally stained glass and beaten copper; Oriental carpets on bare wood floors provided additional glowing colour. These elements are common to all Morris rooms, and his ideas were later adapted and extended to become the style we know as Arts and Crafts.

In his first home, Red House, Morris undertook much of the interior decoration himself, following the mediaeval idea of stencilled ceilings with

THE HIGH-BACKED SOFA IS COVERED IN MORRIS'S 'STRAWBERRY THIEF' FABRIC, A DESIGN STILL AVAILABLE TODAY. THE BIRDS WERE DRAWN BY PHILIP WEBB; MORRIS'S SKILLS AT DEPICTING LEAVES AND FLOWERS DID NOT EXTEND TO DRAWINGS BIRDS AND ANIMALS. IN THE 'ROSSETTI' PAINTING OVER THE FIREPLACE JANEY MORRIS IS AGAIN THE MODEL, THIS TIME AS MARIANA FROM SHAKESPEARE'S MEASURE FOR MEASURE. THE PORTRAIT WAS COPIED BY HELEN SCOTT-LANGLEY USING GOUACHE. A PLATE RACK USED TO DISPLAY ORIENTAL PORCELAIN WAS A FEATURE OF MANY HOUSES DESIGNED BY PHILIP WEBB.

PHOTO COURTESY OF MINI MARVELS.

A MINIATURE CARPET WOVEN IN TURKEY AND REPRODUCED WITH THE GREATEST ATTENTION TO DETAIL. THE PATTERNS OF SUCH CARPETS REFLECT THE STYLES OF DIFFERENT REGIONS; THIS ONE IS A NINETEENTH-CENTURY EAST CAUCASIAN DESIGN. ITS CHOICE FOR THE PARLOUR OF THE DOLLS' HOUSE REFLECTS MORRIS'S KNOWLEDGE OF ORIENTAL CARPETS; HE ADVISED THE VICTORIA AND ALBERT MUSEUM ON SOME OF THEIR PURCHASES.

coloured patterns as a contrast to plain white walls. In that house the effect was enhanced by pieces of oak furniture gloriously hand-painted with mediaeval-style scenes by his friends.

At Kelmscott complementary fabrics and wallpapers were used in some of the bedrooms, although his own preference was always for fabric as a wall hanging. He even hung a huge Oriental carpet over an entire wall and part of a ceiling in one room; this way of displaying carpets never became popular in England, but if the idea appeals to you it would be authentic to include one in a room with plain white walls.

Be careful when using Morris-style wallpapers in miniature rooms: some of the patterns were very bold and could dominate in a small space; choose one of the gentler and smaller patterns. You can use an actual Morris design by carefully trimming and piecing together reproductions from postcards or other sources, but any paper showing Morris influence will give a good effect. Some of Morris's fabric designs are still produced; especially useful for the miniaturist are the patterned fabrics from Liberty intended as dress fabrics, where his designs have been reduced in size.

If your house has enough rooms you can choose to decorate and furnish one of them in the later Arts and Crafts style, using fabrics by Charles Voysey or Arthur Silver. Liberty dress fabrics again include a number of suitable designs printed on fine cotton, which is ideal for both drapes and curtains.

Few people have had such a long-lasting influence on interior decoration as William Morris. A Morris-style room is instantly recognizable and can still seem fresh and new today. Translated into the miniature it has the romantic appeal of the mediaeval combined with more modern ideas on comfort; an irresistible combination.

May Morris embroidered a set of hangings for her father's magnificent oak four-poster bed, and these are still to be seen at Kelmscott. In this miniature version materials resembling the embroidered designs have been used for hangings and coverlet. The poem continues around the valance; the fine lettering was added by Caroline Nisbett.

The large central landing is nicely judged to avoid an abrupt change between the two bedrooms. Morris and his friends enjoyed decorating simple furniture which he designed for his own first home, and the painted chest represents this idea. The watercolour over the chest is of the real Kelmscott, painted by Kenneth Bird, while the reproduction of a Burne-Jones tapestry, now at Standen, is cut from a postcard.

I wanted to include a piece of furniture designed by Charles Rennie Mackintosh in this Morris house; like Morris, Mackintosh's ideas were well ahead of their time. The chair with a stencilled rose design on the back panel was specially made by Felton Miniatures in stained wood, as Mackintosh's preferred strong colours would have been a visual shock against the soft tints of the decorations.

Green ceramic tiles make a superb background for the range. The patterns are replicas of designs by Morris's friend and colleague William de Morgan, produced by Ann Shepley Designs. Miniature versions of other tile designs by de Morgan are used as fireplace surrounds throughout the house.

CHARLES RENNIE MACKINTOSH

THE GLASGOW TOWN HOUSE MADE BY PETER MATTINSON (SEE PAGE 59) IS BASED ON ONE NEAR THE GLASGOW SCHOOL OF ART, PERHAPS MACKINTOSH'S MOST FAMOUS BUILDING. THE DOLLS' HOUSE HAS BEEN DESIGNED AS THOUGH MACKINTOSH HAD BEEN EMPLOYED TO REFURBISH PART OF IT, ALLOWING MORE CONVENTIONAL VICTORIAN FURNITURE TO BE USED IN OTHER ROOMS (AS MIGHT HAVE HAPPENED IN REALITY). THE WALLS OF THIS DINING ROOM ARE STENCILLED IN A ROSE DESIGN ADAPTED FROM ONE BY MACKINTOSH TO SUIT THE SMALL SCALE. THE WHITE BUILT-IN SEAT IS SIMILAR TO ONE IN DUNGLAS CASTLE.

PHOTO COURTESY OF PETER MATTINSON.

Charles Rennie Mackintosh, born 34 years after William Morris, had astonishing talents as an architect, a designer of furniture and an artist. His ideas on houses and room decoration were based on an architectural unity which included not only the house within its landscaped setting but also interior decoration, furniture and fittings down to the last lampshade. His genius has come to be appreciated much more widely today than in his own lifetime.

A Mackintosh room might be difficult to live in. It is most often white and spacious with very little furniture, which is all the more striking for its unique design. Each piece makes a stylistic statement. Nowadays we tend to think of the archetypal Mackintosh chair as black or white, but many of his designs were produced in strong colours – purple and yellow were favourites – which would have made even more impact in those cool white rooms. These are interiors which the art lover will appreciate more than the home owner; there are no squashy sofas, and anyone who has sat on a genuine Mackintosh chair will know that comfort was not his first criterion.

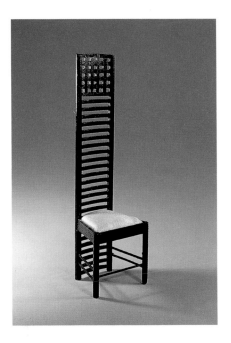

MADE IN GLASGOW BY KAYS MINIATURES, THIS FRAGILE-LOOKING LADDERBACK CHAIR IS EXCEPTIONALLY TALL EVEN BY MACKINTOSH STANDARDS, AND IS INTENDED TO REPRESENT A SLENDER WILLOW TREE. THE ORIGINAL WAS MADE FOR HILL HOUSE.

The prevailing whiteness was softened by the use of elegant stencilled designs used as a border on walls or in leaded stained glass panels set into doors and furniture. A stylized rose is instantly recognizable as his signature. Panels in gesso and metal were the work of his wife, Margaret Macdonald Mackintosh, a considerable artist in her own right. A Mackintosh room is aesthetically satisfying, a work of art with an extra dimension, and in a dolls' house can be breathtaking.

Mackintosh shared with Morris the aim of wanting to bring beauty into everyday life. He too incorporated flower and plant motifs into his designs, but his stylized representations were limited to the rose and the willow tree. The furniture in the Willow Tea Rooms in Sauchiehall Street, Glasgow, is based on a

THE INTRICATE CORNICE IN THIS STARK WHITE BEDROOM IS MASTERLY. THE BEATEN SILVER PANEL ABOVE THE METAL FIREPLACE INCORPORATES AN 'M' MOTIF, REPRODUCED WITH GREAT SKILL IN THIS SMALL SIZE. THE BLACK SETTLE, MADE BY IAN HOLORAN, IS A COPY OF MACKINTOSH'S WILLOW DESIGN; THE LATTICE CONSTRUCTION OF THE BACK REPRESENTS A WILLOW TREE SO STYLIZED THAT IT NEEDS AN ARTIST'S EYE TO RECOGNIZE ITS ORIGIN.

MACKINTOSH WAS STRONGLY INFLUENCED BY JAPANESE IDEAS ON LIGHT AND SHADE; THE DELICATE SCREEN IN THIS MUSIC ROOM ALLOWS A PATTERN OF SHADOWS TO BE REFLECTED THROUGH FROM THE LARGE WINDOW. THE STAINED GLASS IN THE STEEL LIGHT FITTINGS PROVIDES A SMALL TOUCH OF COLOUR.

willow motif ('Sauchiehall' means Alley of Willows).

The designs do not admit of any compromise. It is perhaps for this reason that he did not receive many commissions for complete houses and contents, but fortunately there were enough wealthy patrons willing to commission him to redecorate and furnish individual rooms, perhaps seeking the cachet of a completed design by the internationally famous architect without having to change their whole lifestyle to suit his ultra-modern ideas.

His rooms are not austere in the sense of monkish, but rather in their lack of clutter. Minimalism appeals in principle but not always in practice: we are too fond of our bits and pieces, the things we display in our homes for sentimental reasons or simply because we like them, irrespective of their quality. A complete Mackintosh dolls' house is not for collectors who want to accumulate a variety of miniatures to display in room settings. But we can do the same as his more cautious patrons and have one or two rooms decorated and furnished in Mackintosh style. Recreating a pure artistic concept in miniature is a challenge; properly carried out it will give lasting pleasure.

THE BATHROOM IN THE GLASGOW HOUSE HAS NOT BEEN REDESIGNED BY MACKINTOSH BUT RETAINS EARLY VICTORIAN DETAIL IN THE CORNICING AND CHIMNEYPIECE. THE CUPBOARDS ARE LATER ADDITIONS AND MIGHT HAVE BEEN PUT IN AT THE TURN OF THE CENTURY, SO THEY ARE CONTEMPORARY WITH MACKINTOSH FURNISHINGS.

PHOTO COURTESY OF PETER MATTINSON.

THE 1920s AND 1930s

The 1920s are just far back enough in time to have an aura of glamour which catches the imagination. As a reaction to the Great War of the previous decade, it was a time of renewed social activity; there were all kinds of innovations to be enjoyed – the wireless, the gramophone, the telephone and 'the motor' were still novelties. Decorations and furnishings were influenced by stage sets for the newly popular musical comedies, and the younger generation wanted to play the piano, dance and have fun. Life had changed, and so did ideas on interior decoration.

Alongside this desire for modernity there was also a wave of nostalgia for an apparently safe and solid world which no longer existed, and in some places – suburban England in particular – mock-Tudor and the olde-worlde interior held sway. The two sharply differing styles often co-existed in the same house: for some curious reason it was usually the dining room that became a pastiche of the antique while the lounge would be more modern-looking, decorated in pale colours and sometimes containing avant-garde chrome furniture placed side by side with the traditional sofa and armchairs.

Decorative pottery in Art Deco designs livened up these pastel rooms. Lighting was improved and made more decorative: a standard lamp with slender chrome stem might be placed near the piano to shed light on music, and table lamps were adapted from Chinese vases and topped with shades trimmed with bobble fringe. Keen to keep up with changing styles decoration, many country house owners set about altering the int

IN THE DOLLS' HOUSE THE DECORATION OF THE INSIDE CAN REFLECT CHANGING TASTES IN A HOUSE OF ANY PERIOD. THIS HOUSE, BASED ROUGHLY ON GEORGIAN STYLE, HAS THE ATTRACTIVE CUPBOARD-FRONT OPENING FASTENED WITH A BRASS HANDLE, WHICH WAS A FEATURE OF MANY ANTIQUE DOLLS' HOUSES. IT WAS DESIGNED FOR USE SOLELY AS A DOLLS' HOUSE AND WAS NEVER INTENDED TO BE AN ARCHITECTURALLY ACCURATE MODEL. THE FRONT DOOR IS IMPOSING, AND A HAND-PAINTED CHINA NAMEPLATE HAS BEEN ADDED. THE USE OF MATCHING BLINDS AT ALL THE WINDOWS GIVES THE FAÇADE AN ATTRACTIVELY UNIFORM APPEARANCE.

THESE DELIGHTFUL MINIATURE VERSIONS OF ART DECO POTTERY BY MURIEL HOPWOOD WOULD BE PERFECT FOR THE 1930s DOLLS' HOUSE; THEY ARE BASED ON DESIGNS BY CLARICE CLIFF.

PHOTO BY BOB HOPWOOD.

arrangements while leaving the outside alone, and found that old and new blended together well. So a 1920s or 1930s period interior is perfectly suitable in a Victorian, Georgian or even Tudor dolls' house. The sort of look to aim for is described in many of the cult novels written in this period.

FAÇADE/CONSTRUCTION

The ultra-modern home had its devotees, but many more people were moving into newly constructed mock-Tudor houses or even mock-Tudor flats, albeit with severely modern interiors. Large country houses were designed by leading architects, but their ideas were in general based on vernacular styles, most often Georgian. Although Sir Edwin Lutyens (the builder of Queen Mary's dolls' house) produced many imposing modern public buildings, nearly all his country houses were built for clients who wanted something which would blend in with the English countryside, such as a comfortable adaptation of a mediaeval castle or a manor house.

PHOTO COURTESY OF JEAN BROWN.

THIS LARGE TRIANG HOUSE HAS A GARAGE; CARS WERE AT FIRST OWNED ONLY BY THE RELATIVELY WEALTHY, SO THE SMALLER HOUSES HAD NO NEED FOR A GARAGE. THESE WELL-MADE DOLLS' HOUSES WERE SOLD IN THEIR THOUSANDS UP TO THE MID-TWENTIETH CENTURY. IN MOST CASES THE WALLS WERE PAINTED WITH A FLOWER BORDER OF HOLLYHOCKS ALONG THE FRONT OF THE HOUSE, WHICH ADDED TO THEIR ATTRACTIVE APPEARANCE. UNFORTUNATELY, THEY WERE MADE IN $^{1}/_{16}$ SCALE AND THE ROOMS WERE LOW-CEILINGED, WHICH MAKES FOR PROBLEMS IN REFURBISHING AND FURNISHING ONE OF THESE STILL PLENTIFUL MODELS.

At the same time, the ribbon development of towns and cities produced whole streets of identical three-bedroomed houses with leaded lights in the windows and non-functional beams on the façades. The Triang dolls' houses made from the 1920s onwards were based on these houses, which became known as 'stockbroker Tudor'. Houses with white-rendered walls and either a flat roof or green pantiles and curved metal-framed windows were rarer, and fewer dolls' houses were made in these styles.

As we get nearer to the present day, many people prefer to live in older houses which are changed internally to suit modern taste. You can reproduce 1920s living arrangements in a dolls' house of any earlier period, leaving the exterior exactly as it would have been when newly built; the element of surprise when the house is opened will be all the greater.

INTERIOR FEATURES

The 1920s encompassed many different styles of decor, often mixed with gay abandon. Those in favour of recreating the olde-worlde were kept busy installing period details: windows were cross-hatched with leaded lights; doors were grained in imitation of old oak, and electric lighting mimicked candles, often topped with shades simulating ancient parchment.

Fireplace styles had changed radically. In a Georgian house the owners kept the original fireplaces, but in a new house there were alternatives. For the neo-Tudor look, a polished brick fireplace with arched grate was preferred; it was usual to place a Toby jug copied from an eighteenth-century original in a hearth which in no way resembled its Tudor antecedents. The alternative ultra-modern fireplace style was a fire surround of plain glazed tiles surmounted by a mantelshelf of the kind that was ripped out in thousands in the 1960s.

French windows opened on to the garden at the back of the house. It is unusual to have a back door in a dolls' house, but a trompe l'oeil back way out can be made. All you need is a suitably sized picture of a garden view cut from a greetings card. To make it appear realistic it should be given a wooden door surround to stand out in relief before it. This effect is enhanced by making a step up to the 'open door'.

THIS LARGE ROOM HAS BEEN FURNISHED AS A HALL–'LOUNGE', AN IDEA THAT WAS STRONGLY RECOMMENDED IN HOME INTEREST MAGAZINES OF THE TIME. LARGE SUBURBAN HOUSES WERE OFTEN BUILT WITH A SQUARE HALL WHICH COULD BE USED AS AN EXTRA ROOM, ALTHOUGH THIS PRACTICE WAS GRADUALLY ABANDONED; ADEQUATE HEATING WAS STILL RARE IN PRIVATE HOUSES, AND DRAUGHTS WHISTLED THROUGH THE FRONT DOOR AND UP THE STAIRCASE, WHICH INVARIABLY LED OFF THE HALL. THE BABY GRAND PIANO IS THE PIÈCE DE RÉSISTANCE IN THIS LOUNGE: THE INSTRUMENT WAS DEVELOPED IN RESPONSE TO A GENERAL DESIRE TO HAVE A PIANO IN ROOMS WHICH WERE TOO SMALL FOR THE FULL-SIZE CONCERT GRAND. AN UPRIGHT PIANO WAS CONSIDERED PLEBIAN AT THIS TIME, ALTHOUGH IT MIGHT BE ACCEPTABLE IF IT WERE WHITE OR SHINY BLACK.

INTERIOR DECORATION

In the neo-Tudor environment the picture rail was no longer needed: instead, narrow wooden shelves were often put in near the tops of the walls to hold an assortment of decorative plates and vases. This is an effective idea for the dolls' house and gives the chance to show off a collection of miniature pottery or porcelain.

After a time people began to tire of too much dark oak, and cream-painted woodwork became almost standard in middle-class homes. Walls, too, were painted cream, although light blue or pale green (always referred to as 'eau de nil') were alternatives. In the dolls' house a prettier effect can be achieved by using a pastel wallpaper with a small design in blue or green on a cream ground. Curtains were patterned floral or modern Bauhaus-influenced designs, usually sill-length. A large carpet square of Turkish design left a surround of bare floorboards which were stained and polished.

People were still undecided whether they wanted to have a cottagey interior or to be ultra-modern and chic. The resulting mixture of period styles frequently included some 'Queen Anne' furniture. Many pieces of reproduction furniture, and indeed many houses, were referred to as 'Queen Anne', when in fact they were nothing of the sort. This monarch reigned for only 12 years, so most people were not quite sure what type of furniture had been popular at the time. However, in the 1920s and 1930s 'Queen Anne' meant anything made in walnut and with cabriole legs.

LOUNGE

Spurred on by demand, many craftspeople have become interested in reproducing the furniture of the 1920s in miniature. Although there is not as much available as there is of Georgian furniture, the selection is large enough for those attracted to this period to search out and arrange a dolls' house interior that is delightfully evocative of a set for a Noël Coward play.

The lounge was furnished with comfortable sofas and chairs covered in cut velvet, flower-strewn fabric or a modernistic design according to taste. A wireless embellished by a fretwork screen over its loudspeaker had its own table so that the family could gather round to 'listen in', much as we now sit and watch television. However, the essential ingredient in the 1920s interior is the baby grand piano (*see* page 86). When not in use, its top would be covered by a silk-embroidered Chinese shawl to protect it from the effects of sunlight.

Modern cleaning equipment began to replace the disappearing servant class, and it had become feasible to have pale-coloured carpets. The new, chic ideas were always tried out in the lounge, which could now have the luxury of a fitted carpet. If you opt for a pale cream carpet – easily provided in the dolls' house by a piece of fine woollen fabric with a textured weave – you should also

A SMALL LOUNGE: THE FURNITURE INCLUDES A 'QUEEN ANNE' SOFA AND CHAIR AND A CHINESE CARPET, WHILE THE PAINTINGS ON THE WALL DEMONSTRATE AN INTEREST IN MODERN ART. E.F.BENSON'S MAPP AND LUCIA NOVELS WRITTEN IN THE LATE 1920S WERE THE INSPIRATION FOR THIS ROOM SETTING; THE DOLLS, MADE BY JUDITH JAMES, REPRESENT LUCIA AND HER FRIEND GEORGIE, WHO WAS ADDICTED TO NEEDLEPOINT. THEIR CLOTHES ARE BASED ON THOSE WORN IN THE TELEVISION SERIES BASED ON THESE CULT NOVELS.

THE 'WIRELESS' WAS AN INNOVATION THAT SOON BECAME AN ESSENTIAL IN EVERY HOUSE. THIS PERIOD PIECE WAS MADE BY DAVID WADLEY.

SILVER-FRAMED PHOTOGRAPHS, PREFERABLY OF ROYALTY, ADDED A TOUCH OF ONE-UPMANSHIP WHEN PROMINENTLY DISPLAYED.

have a hearthrug to protect it from flying sparks from the fire. Arrange a log fire in the grate with a few tiny sawn-up twigs and some red shiny paper (*see* page 138), and complete the picture with a dog (preferably a retriever) on the hearthrug.

A few photographs in silver frames will add to the period feeling; in the real house they would, if possible, include signed portraits of royalty. Another current decorative idea was to hang plates as well as, or instead of, pictures on the wall.

DINING ROOM

Those who wished to recreate the Tudor era in some part of their home usually selected the dining room for this treatment. There would be an oak refectory table surrounded by solid oak chairs with leather seats pinned with large metal studs, harking back to the time of Oliver Cromwell, and a sideboard resembling an Elizabethan buffet. This allowed for a display of silver or, if that was too expensive, pewter, which was a good substitute and in any case more appropriate to the neo-Tudor look. Large covered pewter or copper meat dishes were ranged on the buffet, or an oak dresser would display pewter or Spode china plates.

A BEAUTIFUL DRESSER IN THE COTSWOLD STYLE PIONEERED BY ERNEST GIMSON AND THE BARNSLEY BROTHERS AT THEIR WORKSHOPS IN SAPPERTON, GLOUCESTERSHIRE, IN THE EARLY TWENTIETH CENTURY. QUALITY AND HANDWORK WERE THEIR GUIDING PRINCIPLES, FOLLOWING THE ARTS AND CRAFTS IDEALS. THE PANELLING ON THIS OAK DRESSER IS TYPICAL OF THE STYLE, WHICH REMAINED POPULAR THROUGHOUT THE 1930S. THE BLUE AND WHITE WILLOW PATTERN DINNER SERVICE IS IN PORCELAIN BY AVON MINIATURES, AND THE SET OF MUGS IS BY PAT VENNING.

Walls were wood-panelled or distempered in the prevailing cream colour. Sometimes the distemper was applied over plaster which was deliberately given a rough finish to create a country feeling, rather like the snow-effect icing on a Christmas cake. This fashion was guaranteed to catch all the dust and was soon abandoned, but might be fun to reproduce in the dolls' house using commercial plaster filler forked up into rough peaks and left to set before painting.

The dining room was usually chilly and only used at mealtimes. However, in the dolls' house it can be made more inviting by laying the table for a meal; there is plenty of dolls' house food and drink available to make it look appealing.

BEDROOM

The decorative scheme for the bedroom was invariably chosen by the mistress of the house. The main bedroom was pretty and feminine, almost always in pale pink. The latest fashion was to have twin beds rather than a double bed; they were covered with fitted bedspreads of chintz or heavy silk material, and were separated even further by placing a bedside cabinet between them. In the unheated British bedroom matching eiderdowns were provided for the winter months. The furniture would generally be a 'Queen Anne' suite in figured walnut.

Built-in furniture was now becoming popular, and in some smaller homes fitted wardrobes replaced the free-standing ones which took up so much space. In the dolls' house bedroom it is convenient to imagine a built-in wardrobe to allow more space for other miniatures; for the same reason, one bed is preferable to two.

THIS PINK AND WHITE BEDROOM WOULD HAVE BEEN MUCH ADMIRED; IT HAS RETAINED THE TRADITIONAL GEORGIAN-STYLE FIREPLACE, AND THE DRESSING TABLE AND MATCHING STOOL ARE IN THE 1920S VERSION OF 'QUEEN ANNE'. THE CANE BED SCATTERED WITH SILK CUSHIONS ADDS A TOUCH OF THE EXOTIC. SMALL ACCESSORIES AROUND THE ROOM INDICATE THAT THE OWNER HAS EXPENSIVE TASTES; THE MATCHING SET OF MAROON LEATHER LUGGAGE IS READY PACKED FOR A TRIP TO LE TOUQUET.

As in the rest of the house, there were two distinct room styles: the second bedroom was more masculine, with either wood-panelled or cream-painted walls and plain green or blue carpet, curtains and fitted bedspreads. It might contain reproduction oak furniture with vaguely Tudor features, or the plain, well designed limed oak which could now be obtained from Heal's. (These designs have been reinterpreted to suit modern taste in real life in the 1990s.)

For the rich, more exotic decorative schemes were possible. Chinese wallpaper panels and lacquer cabinets might be included, or the bed could be painted white and covered with Oriental-looking fabric or satin and a pile of cushions; Hollywood had a lot to answer for.

Most dolls' houses have two bedrooms, and it makes for an interesting interior to reproduce strongly contrasting styles in the adjoining rooms which can be seen together when the house is opened. Craftsman-made furniture which will fit in well with the chosen schemes can be obtained, and appropriate materials can be used for the soft furnishings.

MAID'S ROOM

Many homes no longer had the services of a cook and the mistress had to come to terms with cooking, but a live-in maid was still taken for granted, and a small bed-sitting room was provided for her use. The furniture was simple and

AN ATTIC BEDROOM FOR THE MAID ALSO PROVIDES USEFUL STORAGE FOR SOME OF THE HOUSEHOLD EQUIPMENT. THE HOOVER IS FROM A PERIOD DOLLS' HOUSE; THE NEEDLEPOINT RUGS WOULD PROVIDE SOME COMFORT ON A CHILLY MORNING. THE BED AND CHEST OF DRAWERS WERE MADE FROM KITS BY BARBARA ANNE MINIATURES.

in the dolls' house can be made up from furniture kits in a plain design. A bed and a chest of drawers are sufficient, and a Lloyd Loom-style cane chair looks pretty without being too ostentatious for use by a servant; make a cushion for the seat for extra comfort. The floor would be polished floorboards with a carpet square or rug, and the bedspread a simple counterpane of embossed cotton.

The maid almost invariably seemed to be called Ethel or Gladys, and in many homes she doubled duty as a general servant. She helped with light housework (although a charwoman would come in to 'do the rough') and sometimes took charge of the children for short periods. In the afternoons she donned a frilly white apron and cap over a dark frock and served afternoon tea.

Although in real life the cleaning utensils would have been neatly put away in a cupboard in the kitchen or under the stairs, you can create a delightful room by including miniature versions of domestic items in a corner of the maid's room. If it is large enough it can be combined with a sewing room (*see* page 19), which would have a treadle sewing machine, ironing board, one of the newfangled electric irons and a wooden clothes airer, which was known as a clothes horse. A miniature feather duster and an old-fashioned carpet beater can be hung on the wall, and miniature Hoovers made for use in the dolls' house in the 1930s can still be found on market stalls or in shops specializing in old dolls' house fittings.

HALL, STAIRCASE AND LANDINGS

A favourite maxim of magazines specializing in home decoration in the late 1920s was that the hall must be made warm and welcoming. Oak parquet flooring was favoured, partially covered by a Turkish rug with a deep red background colour. In the less affluent home the floorboards were stained dark oak and the centre covered with a carpet runner, again with deep red predominating.

THE STAIRCASE IN THIS THREE-STOREY DOLLS' HOUSE HAS SPACIOUS LANDINGS WHICH ARE USED FOR THE CONVENTIONAL FURNISHINGS OF THE TIME – A BAROMETER FOR EXAMPLE. THE GREEN AND CREAM STAIRCARPET FASHIONED OUT OF FURNISHING BRAID CONTINUES THE THEME OF THE MAIN ROOMS RATHER THAN THE STANDARD RED-PATTERNED DESIGN, AND AVOIDS TOO SHARP A CONTRAST IN THE ENCLOSED SPACE.

Hall furnishings were stereotyped; most people liked to stick to traditional schemes. However, wages were low and timber was cheap, so the attention to detail in the average home would be prohibitively expensive in more recent times. Oak staircases with balusters or solid oak infill were commonplace; in the dolls' house hall and staircase, light oak-stained wood makes a change from Georgian white.

An oak chest furnished the hall, but if there was insufficient room a semicircular side table could be substituted. A copper jug in winter or a silver rose bowl filled with flowers in summer was placed on top. The walls were decorated with a collection of eighteenth-century sporting prints or the framed watercolours of the amateur artist owner. The new convenience, the telephone, was always in the hall, together with a barometer on the wall.

All these things can set the scene in the dolls' house hall or landings where space permits, and give an immediate feeling of the period.

BATHROOM

At last the bathroom had arrived. You could even have a bath with taps, instead of a geyser which might asphyxiate you or possibly explode; but in most bathrooms a geyser over the bath was a standard fixture. You could have tiled walls – a 'half-tiled bathroom' was the general description, as the tiles covered just over halfway up the wall. They were white with a black and white border of half tiles, but the ubiquitous green and cream was occasionally used here too. British bathrooms of the time were always cold, and the white tiled effect did not help them to feel any warmer – but this need not trouble us in the dolls' house.

THE TELEPHONE WAS ALWAYS PLACED IN THE HALL, AS IT HAD BEEN WHEN IT WAS FIRST INTRODUCED AND MANY PEOPLE WERE WARY OF 'THE INSTRUMENT'. ELDERLY PEOPLE STILL HAD A DISLIKE OF USING THE TELEPHONE AND HAD A TENDENCY TO HAVE SHOUTED CONVERSATIONS, SO THE HALL WAS A PRACTICAL INSTALLATION PLACE. DAVID WADLEY MADE THE TELEPHONE IN EBONY AND IVORY – IT IS $^{13}/_{16}$IN (2CM) HIGH.

THIS DELIGHTFUL BATHROOM HAS ALL THE NECESSITIES FOR A LUXURIOUS BATH, AND A FEW DECORATOR TOUCHES BESIDES. IT IS GIVEN A NAUTICAL AIR BY THE BLUE AND WHITE STRIPED WALLPAPER EDGED WITH THIN PIPING CORD TO MAKE A 'ROPE' BORDER. THE MARBLE FLOOR IS A PHOTOGRAPH OF REAL MARBLE COVERED WITH ACETATE AND GLUED ROUND THE EDGES BEFORE FITTING THE SKIRTING BOARD. A SHELL COLLECTION IS DISPLAYED ON THE WALL, AND THE DOOR INTO THE ROOM IS NON-OPENING; IT IS MADE FROM A KIT AND GLUED ON TO THE WALL TO GIVE AN IMPRESSION THAT IT LEADS TO ANOTHER ROOM OR CORRIDOR BEHIND. THE SLIGHTLY OUT-OF-SCALE BATHROOM SUITE IS AN ORIGINAL 1930s DOLLS' HOUSE SUITE FOUND ON AN ANTIQUE STALL, AND THE HIGH-FLUSH CISTERN IS MADE FROM A KIT.

Fitting out the miniature bathroom is very enjoyable; you can cheat on the tiles by using a dolls' house wallpaper which simulates them. There are some lovely bathroom fittings available: a $^1/_{12}$-scale toilet with a chain that pulls can be made up from a kit (*see* page 93); brass taps can be fitted to the bath, and 'glass' shelves of clear plastic can be supported by brass brackets. There are lots of dolls' house-size bathroom accessories and toiletries available – racks for the bath, razors, soap dish, hot-water bottle, toothpaste, soap, lotions and shampoos, bath salts and much more.

KITCHEN

In this century the changes brought about by modern technology have had far-reaching effects in the home, and nowhere more so than in the kitchen. The 1920s kitchen contained very primitive equipment by today's standards, but in the upper-class home at least there was still a cook. In many homes the mistress now had to use the kitchen herself and so became more interested in its arrangements; as a result, fashion entered this part of the house for the first time. Cream and pale green was almost without exception the standard colour

A CLOTHES AIRER ON A PULLEY IN THE KITCHEN WAS THE NORMAL WAY OF DRYING OFF CLOTHES AFTER IRONING. THIS MINIATURE VERSION CAN BE RAISED AND LOWERED, JUST LIKE THE REAL THING. THE TOWELS HANGING UP TO AIR ARE MADE BY FRINGING SHORT LENGTHS OF WHITE TAPE AND DRAWING ON THE STRIPES WITH A BALLPOINT PEN. IT IS NECESSARY TO IRON IN A FOLD BEFORE HANGING IF THEY ARE NOT TO STICK OUT AT AN UNNATURAL ANGLE. THE CERAMIC SINK IN THE CORNER HAS A WOODEN PLATE RACK SO THAT PLATES CAN BE LEFT TO DRY. THE 'ENAMELLED' STORAGE BINS FOR FLOUR AND SUGAR ARE OF A DESIGN IN COMMON USE AT THE TIME.

scheme of the time – it was thought to be restful, and no doubt had a soothing effect when one was struggling with the new gas cooker.

Kitchens in the average house built at this time were far too small and may have been a factor in the poor reputation of English cooking for years to follow. However, the Aga, introduced into Britain in 1929, quickly became a status symbol – as it still is today – in those kitchens large enough to have one installed (*see* Suppliers on page 162). Agas have since been brought up to date with the introduction of oil- or gas-fired heating systems, but many households still fought a losing battle with the problems of keeping their solid fuel household god alight.

Floors can be quarry-tiled with $^1/_{12}$-scale ceramic tiles, or you might choose to reproduce linoleum by using self-adhesive plastic. Wall-hung cupboards were now used to hold crockery, although the Welsh dresser continued to take pride of place in the country kitchen. The kitchen cabinet (painted green or cream) was a cupboard resembling a bureau in shape, and sometimes had a let-down flap that could be used as an extra table top. Dry goods were stored in the closed cupboard at the bottom, while china or glass was on show through the glass doors of the top cupboard.

THE COUNTRY COTTAGE

Most city dwellers hanker after a country cottage. Whether it is American weatherboard or sixteenth-century English with thatched roof and roses round the door, the principle is the same: we all want a retreat somewhere away from the hustle and bustle of town life, in the peace of the countryside or perhaps near the sea. The reality is not always so idyllic – especially in the middle of winter – but a country cottage in $^1/_{12}$ scale has none of the drawbacks of the real thing. It is also smaller than the average dolls' house, so someone who lives in a compact apartment can indulge themselves.

PHOTO COURTESY OF RUDEIGIN BEAG.

A SCOTTISH COTTAGE MADE BY RUDEIGIN BEAG HAS BLACK PAINTED STONEWORK SHOWING TO ADVANTAGE AGAINST WHITE WALLS, WHICH IN THE ORIGINAL WOULD BE HARLED WITH A RENDERING COMPOSED PARTLY OF CRUSHED SEASHELLS. THE ROOF IS PANTILED AND THE GABLE ENDS ARE FINISHED WITH STONE STEPS, AGAIN PAINTED BLACK, KNOWN AS 'CORBIE STEPS' – 'CORBIE' MEANS 'CROW'.

Until relatively recently the English country cottage was a modest dwelling: the smallest had a single room and walls made of cob, a mixture of clay and straw built up in layers and left to dry out before colour- or whitewashing to keep out the damp. There would be just one small window, an earth floor and a roof of thatch. I have seen just such a sixteenth-century cottage in Dorset, now used as a garden store; it is so small that it seems impossible that a family could have fitted in.

A dolls' house cottage can reflect the romantic image of the country cottage as most of us think of it, but with less spartan living arrangements. You also need to decide whether your cottage is to be a replica of life as it was lived or whether it will reflect your own dream cottage. Either way it will give a great deal of vicarious pleasure and be a rewarding escapist substitute for the real thing.

FAÇADE/CONSTRUCTION

By the eighteenth century most cottages had an upper storey and were becoming more like those we know today. A timber-framed structure with an infill of wattle and daub might have two ground-floor rooms with an attic built into the roof space and either dormer windows peeping through the thatch or a window between the cruck framing on the gable wall. Alternatively, depending on locally available materials, the construction might be of brick or limestone.

It is possible to buy a $^1/_{12}$-scale cottage with realistic thatch, but this can be simulated in a number of different ways by the miniaturist. Depending on the period, slate (*see* page 131) or stone might be preferred, as many cottages had a thatched roof when they were built but were re-roofed at a later date.

THE ORKNEY CHAIR HAS BEEN MADE FOR FAR LONGER THAN ANYONE CAN REMEMBER; THIS MINIATURE IS IN OAK WITH A WOVEN BACK AND SEAT. THE WHOLE CHAIR WOULD ORIGINALLY HAVE BEEN MADE FROM OAT STRAW OR SEA GRASS WOVEN INTO TIGHT BUNDLES TO GIVE STRENGTH, UNLESS THE COTTAGER WAS LUCKY ENOUGH TO FIND SOME DRIFTWOOD WHICH HE COULD RE-USE.

THIS MINIATURE PORCELAIN MADE BY MURIEL HOPWOOD IS BASED ON THE POPULAR SCOTTISH WEMYSS WARE MADE AT THE FIFE POTTERY IN KIRKCALDY FROM THE MID-NINETEENTH CENTURY UNTIL AROUND 1930. IN FULL SIZE THE CHEAP AND CHEERFUL DESIGNS, GUARANTEED TO APPEAL TO THE COTTAGER, WERE MADE OF EARTHENWARE AND WERE ALWAYS DECORATED WITH FRUIT OR FLOWERS PAINTED AS REALISTICALLY AS POSSIBLE. THE PIGS WERE A SPECIALITY, AND SIZES RANGED FROM THE VERY SMALL TO AN ENORMOUS PIG ABOUT 2FT (61CM) TALL, WHICH WAS GENERALLY USED AS A DOORSTOP.

A TRADITIONAL ENGLISH COTTAGE WITH THATCHED ROOF AND PORCH. THATCHING STYLES HAVE MARKED REGIONAL VARIATIONS WHICH ARE INFLUENCED BY THE TYPE OF STRAW OR REED USED. THE ORNAMENTAL RIDGE PATTERNS ARE INDIVIDUAL TO EACH THATCHER WITHIN LOCAL TRADITIONS. THIS COTTAGE, MADE BY GORDON ROSSITER, IS BASED ON ONE BUILT IN THE EARLY SEVENTEENTH CENTURY AND SINCE RESTORED WITH ENLARGED WINDOWS.

PHOTO COURTESY OF RUDEIGIN BEAG.

VILLAGE BUILDINGS IN FIFE, SCOTLAND, WERE THE INSPIRATION FOR RUDEIGIN BEAG'S IMPRESSIVE STONE-FACED COTTAGE AND SHOP-CUM-POST OFFICE. THE ROOF IS HUNG WITH SPLIT STONE SLATES. IT SEEMS LIKELY THAT THE SHOP WAS A CONVERSION FROM AN EXTENSION OUTHOUSE; THE BOW WINDOW HAS BEEN ADDED TO THE SHOP BY THE MINIATURIST. INSIDE THERE IS A DOOR THROUGH FROM THE SHOP TO THE LIVING ROOM OF THE COTTAGE – A BELL ON THE SHOP DOOR WOULD GIVE WARNING OF A POTENTIAL CUSTOMER.

EVERYONE'S IDEA OF THE PERFECT COUNTRY COTTAGE LIVING ROOM. THE OAK BEAM OVER THE FIREPLACE IS DECORATED WITH HORSE BRASSES, AND THE PLATE SHELF HOLDS A COLLECTION OF MINIATURE BLUE AND WHITE POTTERY. THE OAK FURNITURE INCLUDES A ROCKING CHAIR. NOTE THE COTTAGE DOOR WITH ITS Z-FRAME STRUCTURE AND LATCH HOOK HANDLE, AND THE FAKE STAIRCASE LEADING OFF THROUGH AN ARCH AT THE BACK.

There are a number of British craftspeople who make dolls' house cottages based on vernacular styles. Some of these cottages have thatched roofs, some are tiled; they can be of simulated brick or of cob with white rendering. Often there is an exterior chimney breast or a catslide roof – a feature which extends the sloping roof on one side almost to ground level. The windows are always small. You can have the clean, tidy, updated cottage you might prefer to live in, or one that looks ancient and realistically decrepit.

Inside, the original staircase was no more than a rough ladder with a hole in the upper floor to give access. A small scullery or washroom was sometimes provided in a lean-to extension next to the kitchen/living room. Many dolls' house cottages have better finished stairs than the originals, and some will include the inglenook fireplace which was essential for both heating and cooking.

INTERIOR DECORATION

Interior decoration is much simpler than in a large house; plain white or cream walls look best in the small rooms, and the rustic style calls for uncarpeted, polished floorboards and country furniture. The traditional English country cottage often contains oak furniture, chintz curtains and some antique accessories. The most acceptable form of seating is the Windsor chair, which has been popular in cottage rooms since the seventeenth century.

The larger cottage can have a flagstoned floor in the scullery or kitchen, with a stone sink on brick piers and a kitchen dresser to hold an assortment of crockery. Brass and copper utensils, pottery and pots of flowers in a corner or on a windowsill all reinforce the country look.

PHOTO COURTESY OF BORCRAFT MINIATURES.

PHOTO COURTESY OF DAVID BOOTH.

THREE DISTINCTIVE DESIGNS OF WINDSOR CHAIR, BEAUTIFULLY MADE BY DAVID BOOTH. THE BOW-BACK CHAIR WITH PIERCED BACK SPLAT WOULD DATE FROM ABOUT 1780. THE TALL LATH-BACK STYLE AND THE LOW-BACKED CHAIR WITH TURNED SPINDLES, KNOWN AS A SMOKER'S BOW, BOTH DEVELOPED DURING THE NINETEENTH CENTURY. THE LEGS AND BACK SPINDLES OF A WINDSOR CHAIR ARE ALWAYS DOWELLED INTO THE WOODEN SEAT, AND THERE ARE STRETCHERS BETWEEN THE LEGS.

STURDY POTTERY IS NEEDED FOR EVERYDAY USE IN A COTTAGE. PUZZLE JUGS HAVE ALWAYS APPEALED TO THE RUSTIC SENSE OF HUMOUR, AND THE BLUE JUG MODELLED TO RESEMBLE A FISH WOULD BE QUITE DIFFICULT TO DRINK FROM WITHOUT A SPILL. BRYNTOR MINIATURES BASED THIS DESIGN ON A NINETEENTH-CENTURY ORIGINAL. THE DECORATED CHINA SHELL AND THE ROLLING PIN WOULD HAVE BEEN PRESENTS BROUGHT HOME BY A SAILOR FOR HIS SWEETHEART. THE BEST SET OF CHINA WOULD BE A TREASURED POSSESSION, KEPT IN A GLASS-FRONTED CABINET AND SELDOM USED.

As an alternative, consider a cottage interior which has been updated to show the best sort of modern conversion; again, plain, pale walls will be most suitable, perhaps with a stencilled border. The furniture can be the miniature equivalent of stripped pine, and two or three modern paintings will add colour to the bare walls. Floorboards can be waxed but left pale, and a brightly coloured woven rug will look cheerful.

The American weekend home is often a small timber house which is simply furnished in a similar way. A dolls' house version can be made entirely of wood or adapted by wood cladding both inside and out, using veneer strips. In a corner fishing rods and lines and creels – with or without fish – would suggest the weekend activities. Add a collection of miniature duck decoys or baskets and some well-filled bookshelves for holiday reading.

Many Americans still hanker after a traditional English cottage as their regular weekend home; the next best thing is to own a miniature version. To fulfil such a role it would not be complete without its garden filled with English flowers, and if possible with a wishing well. There are plenty of such cottages to be seen in Wessex and the West Country and in the Shakespeare country around Stratford-upon-Avon, just ready to be photographed on a trip to England and then miniaturized.

PHOTO COURTESY OF GLENDA CAVANAUGH.

PHOTO COURTESY OF GLENDA CAVANAUGH.

IGMA MEMBER GLENDA CAVANAUGH SPECIALIZES IN MINIATURE THATCHED COTTAGES IN ALL THE REGULAR SCALES, BASED ON ORIGINALS SEEN ON HER TRIPS TO ENGLAND. THIS STORYBOOK COTTAGE WITH ITS ECCENTRIC THATCHED ROOF IS IN $^1/_{48}$ SCALE, WHICH IS INCREASINGLY POPULAR WITH AMERICAN COLLECTORS. FOLLOWING THE AMERICAN TRADITION IN DOLLS' HOUSE MAKING (SEE PAGE 10) THERE IS NO FIXED BACK AND THE ROOMS CAN BE VIEWED WITHOUT THE NEED FOR A HINGED OPENING. FITTING OUT THE INTERIOR MIGHT SEEM IMPOSSIBLE IN 1/48 SCALE, BUT HERE THE IMPOSSIBLE HAS BEEN ACHIEVED. LIGHTING IS ALSO PROVIDED.

THE DOLLS' HOUSE SHOP

Dolls' house shops are always popular with collectors who enjoy miniatures without wanting to furnish a complete house. There are some delightful architectural styles available, from country store to elegant Edwardian. A shop can be arranged to display a specialist collection of small treasures or a diversity of objects and furnishings of different periods.

An antique shop is particularly useful for the collector, as it has the advantage that the stock can change, and miniatures for a future project can be displayed attractively and kept safely at the same time. Anyone fortunate enough to visit the Carlisle Collection of Miniature Rooms at Nunnington Hall in Yorkshire (in the care of the National Trust) will enjoy seeing Mrs Carlisle's antique shop. It was commissioned in 1962 to house some exquisite items from her huge collection of miniatures which could not be fitted in elsewhere, and is a wonderful example of how to arrange such a shop to best advantage.

An antiques shop can be laid out formally or as an interesting jumble, and can include such diverse wares as old lace and period clothes, books and musical instruments, teddy bears and Victorian toys, china and furniture; in fact, anything that could be classified as vintage can become part of the shop.

THE SHOP OWNER PROBABLY LIVED UPSTAIRS IN THE ORIGINAL OF THIS TINY GEORGIAN SHOP. MAKER CHRISTOPHER COLE SIMPLIFIED THE ARCHITECTURAL FEATURES OF THE FAÇADE TO SUIT HIS CHOSEN $1/16$ SCALE, AND USED STRONGLY CONTRASTING PAINTWORK TO EMPHASIZE THE DETAILING. THE DOLLS' HOUSE OWNER HAS ADDED A LIFEBELT HANGING NEAR THE WINDOW TO SUIT THE IMAGINED OWNER OF THE SHOP, A RETIRED SEA CAPTAIN.

THE ANTIQUES SHOP IS THE SETTING FOR A DIVERSITY OF FASCINATING OBJECTS: PORCELAIN, SILVER AND BYGONES ARE DISPLAYED ON CHESTS OF DRAWERS AND TABLES, JUST AS THEY WOULD BE IN A REAL ANTIQUES SHOP. OIL PAINTINGS AND WATERCOLOURS ARE HUNG IN A VARIETY OF ATTRACTIVE FRAMES, AS THERE IS NO NEED TO FOLLOW THROUGH A CONSISTENT DECORATIVE THEME. BOOKS, CHINA AND TREEN FILL THE DISPLAY SHELVES TO OVERFLOWING.

THE FOOD STORE

THE CO-OPERATIVE STORE, ALWAYS KNOWN AS THE CO-OP, IS A NATIONAL INSTITUTION WHICH BEGAN IN THE NORTH OF ENGLAND IN A TIME OF HARDSHIP AND HAS PROSPERED EVER SINCE. MOST TOWNS OF ANY SIZE HAVE AT LEAST ONE CO-OP SHOP. RAY AND CHRISTINE LINCOLN SPECIALIZE IN MAKING REPLICAS OF SHOPS COMPLETE WITH SHELVING, COUNTERS AND MOUTHWATERING FOOD ATTRACTIVELY DISPLAYED.

Victorian makers of dolls' house shops liked to reproduce a butcher's hung with realistic looking joints of meat and provide it with a shopkeeper and butcher's boy holding a cleaver at the ready; there are two examples at the Bethnal Green Museum of Childhood in London. To modern enthusiasts it may seem odd and even a little repellent that of all the attractive items sold in shops, the butcher's should have been chosen as a children's toy.

However, many people are attracted by dolls' house food, and for them a grocer's, baker's or general store is probably the best way to display it. If you also enjoy making miniature food you will be able to create your own stock. Alternatively, as with everything else in the dolls' house world, there are specialists who have developed this craft to a fine art.

PHOTO COURTESY OF RAY AND CHRISTINE LINCOLN.

PHOTO COURTESY OF BORCRAFT MINIATURES.

THE TOY SHOP

Many craftspeople enjoy making miniature toys. The smallest are made in cast metal and then hand-painted, as it would be impossible to carve the tiny details in wood. The Victorian rocking horse makes an eyecatching centrepiece for a toy shop display, and although they were not made until early this century, miniature teddy bears are irresistible, whatever the period of the building.

OTHER SHOPS

Some special dolls' house shops are copies of famous originals. Heal's, the innovative furniture store in London's Tottenham Court Road, is well known, but not everyone knows that the first owner of this family-run store, John Harris Heal, was a bedding manufacturer who set up in business in 1818. The

BORCRAFT MINIATURES' REALISTIC TOY SHOP IS FILLED WITH TOYS OF EVERY DESCRIPTION. THIS SPECIAL THEME IS ENHANCED BY THE CONTRAST BETWEEN INTERIOR 'STILL LIFE' AND THE ACTION IN THE STREET OUTSIDE. A SHOP COULD BECOME A LIFETIME HOBBY FOR SOMEONE WITH AN INTEREST IN A PARTICULAR SPECIALITY — THERE WOULD ALWAYS BE ROOM FOR SOMETHING ELSE AMONG THE STOCK.

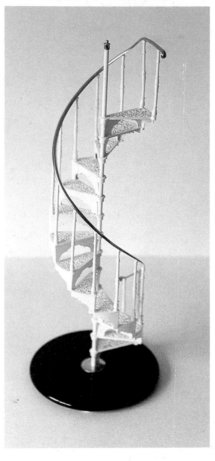

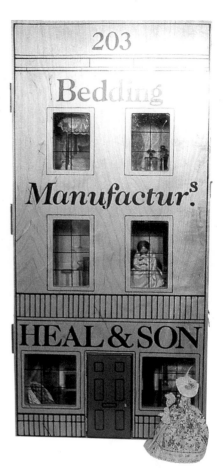

THE WOODEN EXTERIOR OF THIS DOLLS' HOUSE SHOP HAS BEEN VARNISHED TO A SATIN-SMOOTH FINISH TO PROTECT IT WITHOUT OBSCURING THE LETTERING. UNCURTAINED WINDOWS ALLOW A VIEW OF SOME OF THE CONTENTS FROM CLOSE UP – A HEAL'S FOUR-POSTER BED CAN BE GLIMPSED THROUGH ONE OF THE UPPER WINDOWS.

original building was illustrated in Tallis's *London Street Views* in 1838, and during the 1980s Heal's marketed a dolls' house version with a facsimile of the lettering from that first façade on the front.

SHOP FITTINGS

Shops need fittings. An old-fashioned shop counter can be included in a village store, or for a more up-to-date shop, shelving and display cabinets can be built in.

Rather than having a formal staircase in a small shop, a spiral staircase saves space and is delightfully decorative. The miniature version is copied from a Victorian cast-iron original; it can be made to fit any room height and is finished in black or white. An alternative where there is a fixed staircase on a side wall is to fit a rope handrail on the wall and dispense with balusters (*see* page 103). Put in some small gilt picture screws at intervals and thread thin silk picture cord through them.

Attach a small bell to the shop door so that your shop owner has warning when customers come in. Hang it from the top of the door with thin wire, and it will tinkle pleasantly when the door is pushed open. And remember to hang a reversible sign on the door to show whether the shop is 'Open' or 'Closed'.

THIS REPLICA OF A CAST-IRON SPIRAL STAIRCASE IS AN EXACT COPY OF A VICTORIAN ORIGINAL. IT IS MADE IN COPPER-COATED STEEL WHICH IS SPRAY-PAINTED BEFORE THE CURVING BRASS HANDRAIL IS FITTED. JOHN WATKINS HAS DESIGNED THE TREADS AND CENTRE SUPPORT IN SUCH A WAY THAT THE STAIRCASE CAN BE ADJUSTED EXACTLY TO FIT A VARIETY OF ROOM HEIGHTS. $^1/_{12}$ OR $^1/_{16}$ SCALE CAN BE MADE TO ORDER.

THE DOLLS' HOUSE GARDEN

MINIATURE GARDENS EXPERT GEORGINA STEEDS CREATED THIS FORMAL GARDEN SURROUNDED BY NEATLY CLIPPED TOPIARY. IT HAS ALL THE ELEMENTS OF GOOD TOWN GARDEN DESIGN: SYMMETRY, AN ENCLOSED SPACE WITH TREES IN THE BACKGROUND TO SUGGEST THAT THERE IS SOMETHING BEHIND THE HEDGE, AND EVEN THE ILLUSION OF A LONG VISTA WITH A SMALL LEAD STATUE AT THE OTHER END. THE BRIGHT COLOURS OF THE PLANTS AND FLOWERS IN TERRACOTTA CONTAINERS CONTRAST BEAUTIFULLY WITH THE DARK GREEN OF THE HEDGE.

Today's dolls' house no longer has to be contained within four walls, but can be extended to include a garden room or potting shed, a lawn with a sundial, garden ornaments or statuary, and many species of garden flowers. It is rarely possible to arrange a garden large enough to match the size of the building, and in any case the main opening of the house must be accessible. Even so, there is a lot that the garden enthusiast can do to make an attractive setting.

Fashions in garden design have changed over the centuries to suit current building styles, and it is essential to consider the period of your house when planning its surroundings. You can create the suggestion of a garden with just a few miniature flowers and shrubs and a garden seat, or place the house on a baseboard and construct a landscaped garden, introducing features that complement your chosen period. An American dolls' house with an open back can have a front garden, while the British house may have the main garden at the side.

PHOTO BY LIZ EDDISON.

YOU CAN ALMOST SMELL THE APPLES IN THIS OUTHOUSE, WHICH CONTAINS ALL THE EQUIPMENT NEEDED FOR CIDER MAKING. IT WAS CREATED BY W. AND D. KITCHING TO INCLUDE THE WORK OF MANY MINIATURISTS IN A DELIGHTFULLY ATMOSPHERIC AND UNUSUAL SETTING.

The Tudor house could have a knot or herb garden with green plants arranged in a formal design. A Regency or Georgian house might have urns filled with trailing plants on either side of the front door. The Victorian town house can extend into the outdoors with a small garden enclosed by railings. The modern house might have a clipped bay tree in a terracotta pot, and the country cottage a neat vegetable patch or a ceramic sink filled with colourful flowers.

For the larger dolls' house you can provide a variety of interesting features in the 'grounds'. A dovecote or a piece of sculpture could make the centrepiece, and rose arbours, 'stone' seats with lion supports and even working fountains are available. For the smaller garden you could choose a wishing well or a birdbath.

CONSERVATORY

A conservatory makes an elegant addition to a dolls' house, and if built on to the house wall could also be used as a dining room to extend the house into the garden; this is a convenient and pretty way of making a fully furnished dolls' house larger. For the Victorian house it can be furnished with 'cast-iron' chairs and tables and a selection of green plants, ferns and flowers. For the Edwardian conservatory, cane chairs and tables are more suitable.

MANY DOLLS' HOUSES WILL BENEFIT FROM THE ADDITION OF A LEAN-TO CONSERVATORY AT THE SIDE, ENABLING YOU TO EXTEND YOUR MINIATURE WORLD WITH A SMALL PATIO. THE GARDEN SEAT WAS SUPPLIED BY WORLD OF MY OWN. TERRACOTTA POTS FOR MINI-GARDENS ARE MADE IN A VARIETY OF SHAPES AND SIZES BY MINIATURIST POTTERS, AND POTS AND PLANTERS IN CAST RESIN CAN BE PAINTED TO SIMULATE TERRACOTTA OR STONE.

PHOTO BY LIZ EDDISON.

THE MINIATURE VERSION OF VICTORIAN CAST-IRON FURNITURE LOOKS EXCEPTIONALLY DECORATIVE FINISHED IN WHITE. THE TABLE AND CHAIRS ARE EXACT COPIES OF SOME SEEN IN A PUB GARDEN. THE TABLE TOP IS MADE FROM CAST RESIN TO SIMULATE MARBLE – IT IS LIGHT IN WEIGHT AND REALISTIC. THE FURNITURE IS MADE BY JOHN WATKINS IN BLACK OR WHITE.

Create a garden atmosphere with lots of plants. You can make a selection of ferns very quickly by trimming gardener's plant ties to shape; no painting is required. Dolls' house shops will have a range of beautifully made flowers, terracotta plant pots and containers and hanging baskets.

GARDEN ROOM

For those without such wide horticultural ambitions, a garden room inside the dolls' house or as a separate small building will give an opportunity to try out unusual floral decorations and different furniture.

The Georgian garden room was a one-room building which was a feature of a large park surrounding a gentleman's country house. Even the smallest rooms were usually provided with a marble fireplace, decorative cornices, skirting boards and niches for statuary. Larger garden rooms were sometimes used as outdoor summer dining rooms.

Garden rooms enjoyed a revival in the Edwardian era, and their popularity continued until the 1930s. The Edwardian or 1920s garden room can be furnished with cane or wicker table and chairs and a selection of colourful potted plants and ferns. The early twentieth-century garden rooms were used for afternoon tea, as reading or music rooms, or simply as a pleasant place to relax out of the glare of the sun.

PHOTO BY LIZ EDDISON.

A ONE-ROOM DOLLS' HOUSE MAKES THE PERFECT GARDEN ROOM. THIS ONE IS BASED ON A FOLLY SEEN IN THE GROUNDS OF A STATELY HOME. IT BOASTS A GEORGIAN FIREPLACE WITH A BLUE AND WHITE TILED SURROUND (TILES SUPPLIED BY TERRY CURRAN) AND A CRYSTAL CHANDELIER. A TROMPE L'OEIL VIEW HAS BEEN CREATED THROUGH A FAKE DOORWAY IN THE REAR WALL, USING A PICTURE CUT FROM A GREETINGS CARD. THE FURNITURE BY CANE CREATIONS IS REMINISCENT OF THE 1920S, WHEN GARDEN ROOMS ENJOYED A REVIVAL OF POPULARITY – I HAVE SEEN SUCH FURNITURE QUIETLY MOULDERING AWAY IN THE GARDEN BUILDINGS BELONGING TO SEVERAL HISTORIC HOUSES.

GARDENING HINTS

Almost anything you can think of for the well stocked garden is available in the miniature scale. There are, however, a number of things you can make yourself. Start with a baseboard and plan out the features you want to include.

Paths
Sand and gravel-coloured flock powder are available from model railway stockists. Mark out the paths, brush them with glue and sprinkle the flock powder on top. Shake off the surplus and repeat the process to fill any bald patches. Make the paths first, to avoid getting the powder where it is not wanted. Alternatively, you can lay paths using miniature bricks or flagstones.

111

Lawns

Use railway modeller's grass, which is sold in a roll or by the piece; this only needs cutting to shape and gluing down.

Borders

Use earth-coloured flock powder in the same way as for paths. This looks most realistic if the borders are slightly raised by being laid over a base of scrunched-up paper glued on to the baseboard.

Shrubs and trees

Realistic shrubs and trees are available in a variety of colours and types from model railway suppliers, and convincing trailing plants and wall creepers can be made from metal plant kits which come packed flat, ready to be painted and bent into natural shapes. A bay tree is easy to make: just give it a straight stem and a neatly trimmed rounded top made from florists' Oasis, which can be trimmed to shape with a craft knife or scissors.

PHOTO BY LIZ EDDISON.

Vegetable garden

Use a base of corrugated cardboard well covered with 'earth', to which purchased vegetables can be added in neatly spaced rows. Lettuce, cabbage or fruit bushes are all suitable.

Garden pond

A small pond is best made from plastic mirror material which can be cut with scissors. It is safer than glass and has a reflective quality which makes it realistic. Camouflage the edges with plants.

Rockery

Make a bank with papier-mâché, using newspaper and wallpaper paste, the tried and tested schoolroom method. This will take several days to set hard. Make rocks by breaking up bits of polystyrene from reclaimed packaging; paint them a streaky grey-white and fix them on to the bank with polystyrene cement. On a miniature scale this will be more convincing (and lighter in weight) than real stones. Cover the spaces with earth flock powder before adding plants.

Pedestal

Use a wedding cake pillar as a base for a statue, garden ornament or trailing plant.

PART FOUR

PRACTICAL

PHOTO COURTESY OF SAMUEL HALFPENNY (J. NEILL RICHARDSON).

SAMUEL HALFPENNY (J.NEILL RICHARDSON) BUILT VALENTINE COURT FROM SOLID MAHOGANY. THERE ARE 36 ROOMS, 64 WINDOWS, MOSTLY SASH OPENING, AND 700 PANES OF GLASS. THE EXTERIOR IS BEESWAXED TO SHOW THE BEAUTY OF THE WOOD. THIS MANSION SHOWS JUST WHAT CAN BE ACHIEVED AFTER YEARS OF PRACTICE. THE MAKER WORKS SOLELY TO COMMISSION AND WILL ONLY TACKLE A HOUSE WHEN HE FEELS IT TO BE A TEST OF HIS SKILL.

You can achieve a professional finish without any experience of interior design when you decorate a dolls' house. Many people are reluctant do-it-yourselfers, uneasily aware that the painting and wallpapering of their own home is not quite up to the standard they aimed for. But miniature decorating is much simpler: you do not need to have a head for heights or be an expert carpenter; and if you do make a mistake and put the wallpaper on upside down or cut a piece of skirting board shorter than is needed, it will not be prohibitively expensive to start again.

It is not necessary to go to great lengths to reproduce scaled-down versions of building materials; it is often the simplest solution which is the best. The exterior of a plain dolls' house will look more authentic if period details are added, but such features as keystones above windows and quoining on a brick-faced house will give the same effect if made in card, which is easy to cut with scissors, as in wood, which must be cut with a saw.

Like any home, a dolls' house will express the personality of its owner, and it is this individuality which is part of the attraction: no two dolls' house interiors are ever the same. It is the accessories you make yourself to supplement treasured craftsman-made furnishings which will bring the house to life. The practical miniaturist needs to develop the characteristics of a magpie and look out for small objects which can be adapted: small, rigid boxes, chess pieces from old, incomplete sets, cotton reels, beads, old jewellery, ribbon and lace trimmings, cotton tape, wallpaper and carpet samples, metal domes for disguising screw heads – all these and more can be utilized. Keep a box for treasure trove.

Anyone can make stylish accessories, often from unlikely materials, which can form the basis of an authentic looking piece of household equipment or *objet d'art* and help to create a busy, home-like dolls' house.

TOOLS AND THEIR USES

Tools for miniature work are minimal and inexpensive, and their use can be learned very easily. The essentials, which you probably have in your household toolkit already or which can be obtained from the hardware shop or DIY store, are:

✤ A **hammer**

✤ **Pliers** and **pinchers**

✤ A '**gent's saw**' (about 7in or 17.8cm long)

SIMPLE DECORATIONS OFTEN LOOK BEST. THESE SPARSELY FURNISHED GEORGIAN ROOMS ARE FITTED WITH CORNICES, DADO RAILS AND DEEP SKIRTING BOARDS ALL PAINTED WHITE, INSTEAD OF THE DRAB OR DULL GREEN WHICH WERE LIKELY TO HAVE BEEN USED IN THE ORIGINAL HOUSE. THE RESULT IS A LIGHT INTERIOR WHERE THE CONTENTS SHOW UP WELL. THE INSIDE OF THE OPENING FRONT IS PAPERED IN AN ALL-OVER DESIGN (SEE PAGE 146) WITH BORDER DETAILS CUT AND FITTED TO MAKE SURROUNDS FOR WINDOWS AND DOORS.

+ Small **screwdrivers**

+ A **bradawl** (a pointed tool for starting a hole in hardwood)

+ Good quality **paintbrushes** – $\frac{1}{2}$in, $\frac{3}{4}$in and 1in (13mm, 19mm and 25mm) are the most useful

+ Several fine grades of **sandpaper**, 00 to 2, plus the finest grade of **glasspaper**

In addition there are a few specialized items which will be obtainable from a good art shop, a dolls' house supplier or craft shop:

+ A **craft knife** or a **scalpel** fitted with a size 10A blade

+ A **mini-metal ruler with a raised edge** to act as a cutting guide

+ A **metal mitre box and saw** – X-Acto box no. 7533 and knife handle no. 5 fitted with saw blade no. 236 or 239

+ **Fine art paintbrushes** – sizes 000 to 3 are the most useful

As you progress you may find additional tools useful. A **mini-drill**, a **magnifying glass** on a stand and a **fretsaw** are invaluable if you want to extend your talents and try making miniature furniture, and useful when making up kits. A self-healing **cutting mat** with a grid of squares is invaluable, but is expensive if you are unlikely to take on more than one dolls' house.

SAFETY

Remember to use your tools with care, and do not leave them lying about when not in use. The purpose of a saw is to cut. A scalpel will cut to the bone. Always remember to check that your other hand is clear before you cut. Use a safety ruler with a raised edge to cut against, never a wooden ruler. Dig the blade of a craft knife or scalpel into a cork when not in use, and put all tools out of the reach of children.

One point to note is that a scalpel comes without instructions for changing the blade. It is a more effective tool than a craft knife because it is sharper, but the blades do need to be changed frequently. Ask the assistant in the art shop to show you how to do it safely; do not experiment on how to do it without instruction.

MITRE BLOCK AND SAW

In order to fit skirting boards, cornices and other small fixtures, angled joins must be perfect; this cannot be achieved without a mitre block and saw. The

SCISSORS, SCALPEL, METAL RULER WITH RAISED EDGE AND CUTTING MAT.

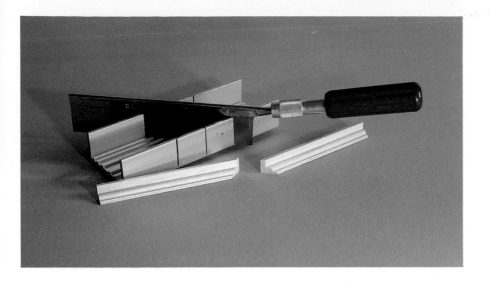

miniaturist's metal mitre block is grooved to take different sizes of small mouldings and hold them firmly, and has a straight-cut slot as well as those for right- and left-angled mitres. Extra saw blades to fit into the knife handle can be bought separately; change the blade as soon as it becomes even a little blunt, as an incorrect blade size will damage the mitre block slots immediately.

ADHESIVES

You will need several different kinds of adhesive. Modern technology has produced specialist glues for specific purposes, and it is essential to use the correct one for the job. The most useful for the dolls' house decorator are:

- ❖ **'All-purpose' clear adhesive** — for card, paper, wood, ceramic.
- ❖ **White wood adhesive** (Evo-Stik Resin 'W') — for *permanent* fixing of wood: once set, the join cannot be undone.
- ❖ **Fabric glue** (Copydex) — to attach fabric to other surfaces; to fix ceramic tiles on to wood.
- ❖ **Impact glue** — to attach metal roof ridging, railings or small parts.
- ❖ **Epoxy resin** (extra-strong all-purpose glue mixed from two tubes before use) — will provide an exceptionally strong bond on small parts, e.g. metal feet fixed to wooden legs.
- ❖ **Polystyrene cement** (unlike other adhesives, this will not dissolve polystyrene) — useful for the dolls' house garden.
- ❖ **Paper glue** (Gloy) — this has limited use, as it is easy to over-wet paper and leave a crinkled effect; use on thick paper only.
- ❖ **Wallpaper paste**

BUILDING A DOLLS' HOUSE

For those with carpentry skills who want to build their own dolls' house, it is worth making a thorough investigation and looking at as many dolls' houses by successful makers as you can before you begin work. Plans for dolls' houses are also available from professional dolls' house designers and some dolls' house shops.

Bear in mind that the scale is important and that the rooms should not be more than 12in–15in (30cm–38cm) deep, otherwise furnishings at the back of the rooms will be obscured and difficult to reach. ⅜in (10mm) plywood for external walls and ¼in (6mm) plywood for internal walls will give sufficient strength and rigidity; if the house is to be papered or painted you can use medium density fibreboard (MDF).

High quality ready-made windows, doors, staircases and fireplaces can be bought, and if you decide to use these you will need to plan the measurements of your house with care. Bear in mind that a dolls' house has three-sided rooms designed to be looked into from the front, like a stage set.

THIS HOUSE MADE BY TRENT WORKSHOP HAS A NICE VARIETY OF ROOM SIZE. THE STAIRCASE IS AN INTERESTING FEATURE; THE BALUSTERS AND RAIL ON THE LANDINGS CAN BE REMOVED FOR DECORATION. CHIMNEY BREASTS ARE READY FITTED BY THE MAKER ON THE END WALLS IN EACH ROOM.

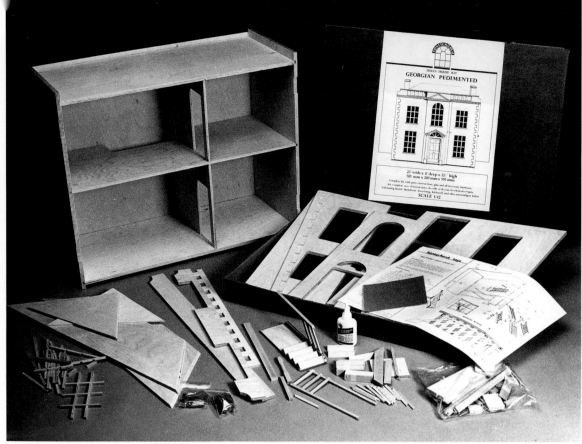

PHOTO COURTESY OF HONEYCHURCH TOYS LTD.

A HOUSE FROM A KIT

One option is to build a house from a kit. There is a wide choice of kits, always at a saving on the fully finished price. Making a large, elaborate dolls' house from a kit is a long process and can be daunting for a beginner or someone with a deadline to meet, so it is sensible to choose a simple design for your first dolls' house. Kits are supplied with detailed assembly instructions; no carpentry skills are needed and only a few tools – a screwdriver, a drill or auger, wood glue, fine sandpaper, masking tape and some clamps for use while the glue is setting.

However clear the instructions, it is not always possible to understand everything at first reading. Read them through carefully and have a dry run before assembly to make sure that you follow the sequence correctly. At the same time you can check the fit and make any fine adjustments so that the wood fits neatly into pre-cut grooves, using a craft knife or fine sandpaper. When using sandpaper, always wrap it around a squared-off piece of wood so that you do not round off the corners; an emery board is useful for fine-finishing grooves or slots.

Sand all the parts with fine glasspaper (size 000) and wipe clean before permanent fixing with white wood glue. Tape or clamp the parts together while the glue sets, which will take several hours until full strength is reached. Check that the walls are joined at right angles: use a plastic set-square for this – they are inexpensive and can be easily obtained from a stationer's. If the house is to be painted it is worth taking the trouble to fill any hairline cracks and sand smooth before undercoating, to give a perfect finish.

A KIT FOR A TWO-STOREY GEORGIAN DOLLS' HOUSE.

119

RESTORATION

In the current wave of enthusiasm for dolls' houses and miniatures, many houses which were temporarily abandoned are being brought out into the light of day once more.

A LINES HOUSE DATING FROM 1910. THE ORIGINAL EXTERIOR HAS BEEN OVERPAINTED IN RED BY A PREVIOUS OWNER; THE BALCONY RAILS WERE INTACT, BUT THE FRONT DOOR AND PART OF THE ROOF WERE MISSING WHEN IT WAS BOUGHT BY JEAN BROWN, WHO HAS RESTORED IT AS DISCREETLY AS POSSIBLE WITHOUT ALTERING THE PRESENT EXTERIOR COLOURS.

PHOTO COURTESY OF JEAN BROWN.

Many families have a dolls' house tucked away in the attic for future use. Sometimes it has been packed up carefully to keep 'for the grandchildren', with its furnishings neatly arranged in boxes. Other houses were put away in whatever state they were in when last played with, and much of the furniture is missing or broken. A rare few have been treasured through several generations, well documented and cared for, and are now of historic interest; families who have such a dolls' house are exceptionally lucky.

If you do not own a family dolls' house but would like to try your hand at restoration, it is sometimes possible to buy a dilapidated house in need of updating at a sale or even in a junk shop or street market. Some of today's foremost makers started in this way.

But a word of caution before you start searching: in the past, many amateur carpenters have made dolls' houses for their children, sometimes from the roughest of materials. Although you might pick up an old home-made house to practise on for a small sum, examine it carefully before you buy. If it has been made from old tea chests or poor quality wood which is too thick for the purpose, with no consideration given to scale or architectural style, you are not going to be satisfied with it when restored, however precise your work.

A SUCCESSFUL TUDOR HOUSE CONVERTED FROM A BATTERED HOME-MADE HOUSE. THE WALLS ARE PLASTERED AND HALF-TIMBERING, NOT PART OF THE ORIGINAL STRUCTURE, HAS BEEN GLUED ON TO THE PLASTERED SURFACE. THE LATTICE-PANED WIDOWS WERE SUPPLIED BY WENTWAYS MINIATURES. A NEW FRONT DOOR HAS BEEN FITTED. THATCH IS LAID OVER THE ORIGINAL ROOF, CARE BEING TAKEN TO ROUND OFF THE CORNERS AND FOLLOW A TRADITIONAL RIDGE PATTERN. FINALLY, THE DETAILED PROFESSIONALLY MADE TUDOR CHIMNEY BY GORDON ROSSITER REPLACES THE BLOCK OF WOOD WHICH WAS THE TOKEN CHIMNEY BEFORE THE HOUSE WAS RESTORED AND IMPROVED.

PREPARATION

Most of the structural and decorative ideas given in the following pages are also applicable in restoration; however, if you suspect that the house is a genuine period piece dating from before 1920, do nothing to it until you have sought expert advice, perhaps from your local museum curator or a specialist dolls' house or collectors' magazine (*see* page 168). It would be sad to find that you had 'restored' a genuine antique which would have been of greater interest and perhaps more valuable if left in its untouched state.

The house must first be put in order, and an old dolls' house can be in a very sorry state, with damaged roof and scratched windows, broken woodwork and unsuitable paint. The house which I found in an antiques market was in this condition, and at first sight seemed unpromising with its bright orange paintwork, green and much battered roof, and one side hanging off. But there were several features which made me take a second look. The wood itself was good; it had a wide staircase and the holes roughly cut for windows were right for a conversion to Tudor, something I wanted to try out.

The size and shape of windows is crucial to period styles – a front door can be altered or replaced and small windows enlarged and fitted with the correct type of glazing and glazing bars, but if the windows are too large there is little that can be done beyond making a complete new front for the house.

Begin your restoration by washing the house thoroughly with warm water and detergent. It is best to do this out of doors if possible, as it is a messy task if there is old wallpaper and carpeting to be removed. Wallpaper can be taken off fairly easily once it has been wetted thoroughly, but you may have to persist if extra-strong glue has been used. Carpet that has been glued firmly into place can be more difficult. Try to find out what type of glue has been used by testing different solvents on a small patch. White spirit often works well, and wire wool will help to remove the last traces of fluff and threads from the floors.

Some old dolls' houses, particularly the home-made variety, will have been painted both inside and out with old-fashioned oil-based paints which are too thick and shiny and often in unsuitable colours. Here there is no alternative but to strip off at least the top layer of paint and then check what is underneath before you continue. Use a commercial paint stripper, wear rubber gloves if you value your hands, and follow the instructions.

A small wire brush is useful for stripping off the paint, and for corners you may find it helpful to use an orange stick or a knitting needle to remove flakes of half-dissolved paints. This is a job which should also be tackled in the open air, or at least in a well ventilated room with the windows open and a through draught. When all the paint has been removed, wipe the house over with white spirit and leave it to air – the smell will soon disappear and the wood will then be in a clean state, ready for restoration.

REPAIRS

The next step is to repair or replace broken parts of the structure. If your house opens like a cupboard, check to see whether the opening front has sunk on its hinges, which may need adjustment or replacement. The windows may not be correctly proportioned, and you may have to use a fretsaw to cut them a little larger or to turn square windows into rectangular ones. The front door may be missing or incorrect for the period, and you may want to replace it with something more suitable. Remember when fitting a new door to allow clearance for any floor covering which may go in later on.

Many houses made in the early twentieth century were provided with metal window frames and doors, as these were supplied as standard on commercially made dolls' houses and were also available from hobbies shops for use by the amateur dolls' house maker. The metal window frames were sometimes fitted with small hinges so that the windows could open and close; children enjoyed this realism, and many such windows became bent and twisted after much play. The celluloid 'glazing' also had a tendency to turn yellow, and became opaque or scratched.

You may find it best to replace damaged windows and frames. It is still possible to obtain this kind of window in standard sizes. Alternatively, replace the glazing by the method described on pages 143 and 144.

PHOTO COURTESY OF JEAN BROWN.

HALFWAY THROUGH THE RESTORATION OF THE FAÇADE OF THE LINES HOUSE.

Commercially made dolls' houses were sometimes provided with a roof covered with a thick cardboard ply which was painted and scored to simulate red roof tiles, and this was easily damaged at the corners. The roof can be repaired by carefully separating out the damaged layers and gluing them back together, if necessary adding an extra piece which will need to be taped in place for extra strength, as well as being glued. It is then best to cover the entire surface with new 'slates' by one of the methods shown on pages 131 and 132.

None of these repairs is difficult for the amateur with a little patience, but they need to be done early on; once the house is in order you are free to continue with the decoration and furnishing. You may choose to follow the original schemes, if these are known, or to follow your own ideas. Either way, the restoration of a dilapidated dolls' house is an interesting and rewarding task.

Lighting

Lighting is an attractive option, but bear in mind that it will need a certain amount of maintenance. As in real life, bulbs last for a limited time and have to be replaced occasionally. And if something does go wrong with the wiring after you have carefully concealed it under the wallpaper, you may have to redecorate after you have located the fault.

It is best to install lighting at the construction stage. A professional dolls' house maker will do this by cutting grooves with a router to take the wiring in floors or walls; it can also be done with a carefully shielded rotary saw with a shallow cut. But neither method can be recommended to the amateur without a workshop, and for someone making up a dolls' house from a kit it makes matters unnecessarily complicated. One method is to use copper wiring, which does not require grooves.

Whichever system you choose, check that everything works before you begin decorating, and plan the decorations in conjunction with the wiring, so that if anything goes wrong all the points where the wires or tapes are joined together and where the fittings are joined to the wires are accessible for repair or replacement.

The essentials for lighting are bulbs, wiring, a switch or switches, a connector block, transformer and fuse, or batteries.

TRANSFORMER

This must be matched to the number of bulbs used and their voltage. A 1-amp transformer should be good for up to 20 bulbs, and so is suitable for most dolls' house systems. Some transformers are fitted with a safety cut-out against overloading, or you can wire in a fuse holder with a 12-volt fuse.

BATTERY

A battery has a lower initial cost and no fuse is required. However, it must be checked and replaced periodically, which is an ongoing expense, and in any case a battery is unsuitable if the lighting is to be left on for long periods.

LIGHTING IS ALMOST A NECESSITY IN A REALLY LARGE DOLLS' HOUSE. THE INTERIOR OF THE GLASGOW TOWN HOUSE (SEE PAGE 59) IS ASTONISHINGLY BEAUTIFUL. MAKER PETER MATTINSON PROVIDED MINIATURE VERSIONS OF THE METAL AND COLOURED GLASS FITTINGS TO WHICH MACKINTOSH GAVE SO MUCH ATTENTION.

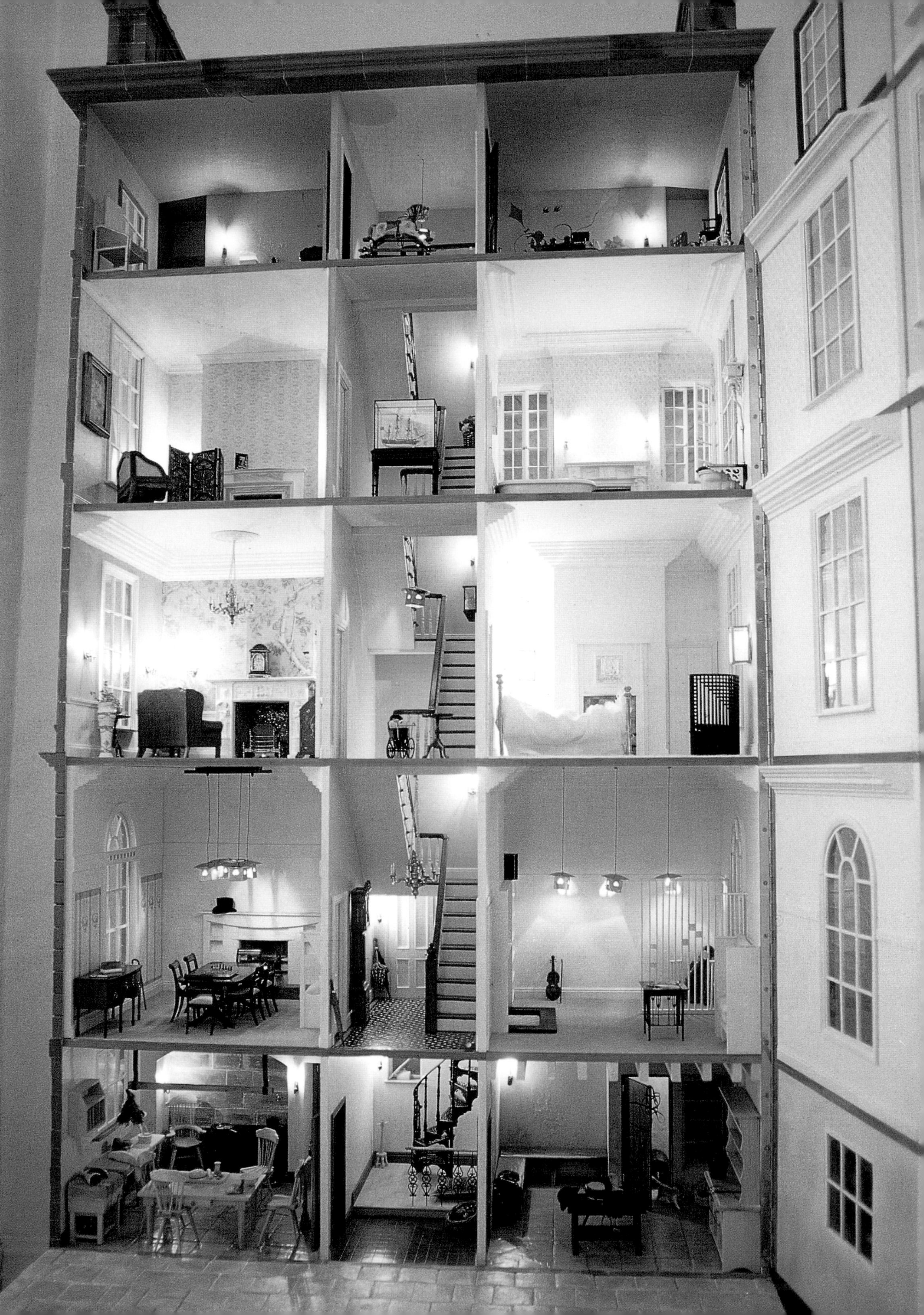

Photo courtesy of Peter Mattinson.

BULBS

There are several types of bulbs which can be used:

'Pea' bulbs (used in torches) are easily available but overlarge, and are made even more obtrusive by the holders they screw into. They are also overbright for the surroundings, but can be replaced easily and are suitable for a dolls' house intended for a child.

LES bulbs (used in Christmas tree lights) are smaller. They also screw into a holder.

'Grain of rice' or 'grain of wheat' bulbs are the neatest, although still not quite as small as a $\frac{1}{12}$-scale bulb should be. These are tiny capless bulbs that have the wires coming directly out of the glass envelope. They need to be soldered into the circuit, which makes changing a bulb difficult. These bulbs will, however, provide low-level, atmospheric lighting suitable for a period interior, and there will be no problems finding shades in the correct scale.

WIRING

Dolls' house lights need to be connected in parallel by a separate pair of wires from each light. These should all be fed from a connector block inside or at the back of the house so that a single pair of wires leads away to the transformer or battery, which can then be out of sight. Copper tape wiring with a self-adhesive backing is easy to fit and can be concealed under ceiling paper or flooring. It is also possible to obtain $\frac{1}{12}$-scale skirting board with a groove ready cut in the back to take wiring, so a combination of copper tape and ordinary wires can be used, soldered together where necessary. Copper tape lighting systems are available as a kit, with full instructions for fitting.

SWITCHES

Switches are not available in a suitable size for a $\frac{1}{12}$-scale room. The smallest are toggle or press-button types from electrical shops. If separate switches are to be used for different rooms, it is best to have all the switches on a separate control board, together with the transformer or battery.

READY-WIRED SYSTEMS

An alternative is to buy a ready-wired system where the bulb holders are wired through a ceiling rose, so all that is necessary is to drill a hole in the ceiling for the wiring, which can be concealed by the floor covering in the room above. This type of system has plenty of wire already fitted to a connector block, so no soldering is required. A lighting kit of this kind is the simplest to fit, but also, of course, the most expensive.

PHOTO COURTESY OF PETER MATTINSON.

VICTORIAN GLASGOW BY NIGHT. LAMPS TO ILLUMINATE THE HOUSE ENTRANCE WERE ESSENTIAL IN BADLY LIT STREETS.

DECORATION

In the world of the dolls' house there are no hard and fast rules about what you can and cannot do. Even so, looking at your wooden shell, whether purchased ready-made, assembled from a kit or all your own work, you may wonder where to begin. There are pitfalls for the unwary, so here are a few suggestions on how to avoid them and how to use your talents as an interior designer to make your dolls' house into something special. To carry your project through successfully requires advance planning; before you do anything to your house stand back and think carefully about the possibilities.

As a general principle it is best to decorate the outside before you begin on the inside, although such details as shutters, windowboxes and porches can be added later. But there is a certain amount of preparation necessary to both exterior and interior which can be done together.

PREPARATION

Rub over the entire house with glasspaper. Remove the dust and then wipe over with white spirit to leave a clean surface for decoration. At this stage you can undercoat both inside and outside. If the house is front-opening you will need to turn it on its back to get at the ceilings properly; support the front openings while the house is in this position, to avoid putting a strain on the hinges, and cover the floors to avoid splashes. A white undercoat is a good idea even if you plan to paper over it, as dolls' house wallpaper is thinner than full-size and is inclined to pick up stains from the wood.

Unless you are planning an unusual ceiling treatment, it simplifies the decorating procedure to topcoat the ceilings at this stage. White will help to reflect light into the rooms, but for a perod feeling you may prefer to use one of the slightly tinted emulsion paints rather than a brilliant modern white. These shades are available in small sample pots for decorators to test the colours, and two of these should be sufficient for all the ceilings in even the largest dolls' house. Never skimp on paint: always apply two coats.

EXTERIOR

The exterior finish needs to be considered in relation to the period style of the house. Dolls' houses can be painted, papered with brick or stone paper, varnished or polished with beeswax to enhance beautiful wood (*see* page 71). There are other exterior finishes appropriate to specific types of houses, and these can be achieved with care and patience.

PHOTO COURTESY OF GARY WARD.

BRICK LAID TO FORM A HERRINGBONE PATTERN MAKES A STUNNING EXTERIOR FINISH FOR THIS TUDOR HOUSE BY GARY WARD. ALTHOUGH FINISHING A WHOLE HOUSE IN THIS WAY WOULD PROBABLY BE TOO MUCH FOR THE AMATEUR TO CONTEMPLATE, IT IS ALSO A TRADITIONAL WAY OF USING BRICK TO LINE AN INGLENOOK FIREPLACE, WHERE IT WILL NOT BE SO TIME-CONSUMING.

Brick can be simulated with careful painting, but it is laborious and quite a difficult art to master. A skilled dolls' house maker will sometimes provide ceramic or wooden brick cladding (*see* page 141).

PAINT FINISHES AND CHOICE OF COLOUR

A pastel colour will resemble the stucco finish on many period houses – soft green, yellow or apricot for a Regency house, and white or stone for Georgian, light grey or blue for Victorian. A house intended for a child can be a bright colour (*see* page 9): a very small house painted a deep red with plenty of white detail can look delightful (*see* page 13). Use eggshell paint, never gloss, and apply two top coats, rubbing down gently between coats.

BRICK OR STONE PAPER

Paint is harder-wearing than paper for the outside of a dolls' house, but if you want to use brick paper choose the best quality that you can find. Use ordinary wallpaper paste and size the walls thoroughly first. The simplest way to deal with the window and door apertures is to paper straight over them. Leave until thoroughly dry and then cut round the edges of the openings using a craft knife or scalpel.

QUOINING

Quoining is an attractive feature of many brick-built houses and can be reproduced easily; it will also protect the edges and corners from damage if the exterior is wallpapered. You will need some firm card about $\frac{1}{4}$in (6mm) thick. Paint it with a coat of white emulsion followed by one coat of white or stone-coloured eggshell paint or matt finish model paint. Make two templates and cut 1in (25mm) squares of card and an equal number cut in half to measure 1in x $\frac{1}{2}$in (25mm x 13mm). You will need enough to glue alternately on to the edges of the front walls.

OTHER EXTERIOR FINISHES

An elegant external finish can be made by leaving the wood in its natural state and waxing or varnishing it to an attractive sheen (*see* pages 114 and 106). A dolls' house might be finished in this way if it is to be displayed in a room with other furniture. Wax polishing needs care and persistence to produce a good finish which will allow the natural grain of the wood to show to advantage.

A satin varnish – never gloss – will also give an excellent finish; care must be taken in applying to make sure that there are no drips – check five minutes after finishing to make sure none has appeared, and brush any in carefully. You will need up to eight coats of varnish rubbed down gently with a soft cloth between coats to produce a translucent sheen which is satin-smooth to the touch.

SPECIAL EFFECTS

Cob Apart from the straightforward painted, papered or polished exterior, other finishes can be achieved with a little time and patience to suit vernacular styles. For the country cottage or Tudor house, plaster over plain wooden walls using commercial plaster filler (Tetrion or Polyfilla) mixed with white wood glue instead of water, with a sprinkling of powdered French chalk. Experiment with a small quantity on a spare piece of wood: a thin layer must cling to the wall without danger of crumbling or falling away; the correct texture will set fairly quickly, producing a plaster finish resembling cob.

A quicker method is to paint with exterior weathershield house paint, but the result is not quite as realistic. As this paint is only sold in large cans, it is expensive unless you happen to have some already opened.

Weatherboarding This is an attractive finish which is common in America but is confined to only a few regions of England; it can be simulated by gluing on $^{1}/_{2}$in (13mm) strips of card (posterboard), which must be cut accurately. Begin at the bottom of each wall, overlapping each strip about $^{1}/_{4}$in (6mm). Finish the corners with a 1in (25mm) strip of card folded down the centre. Weatherboarding can be painted white or stained to retain the natural wood colour.

Pebble dash Houses were often finished with pebble dash in the 1920s and 1930s. To add a touch of authenticity to a small house of this period, reproduce the effect by gluing sheets of fine sandpaper rough side out to the outside walls and painting with white or stone-coloured emulsion paint.

A DECORATOR'S PAINT TESTER POT PROVIDES THE EMULSION UNDERCOAT FOR COLOUR MIXING AND EXPERIMENTING WITH THE TUBES OF GOUACHE.

Cotswold house exterior finish   The Cotswold stone referred to on page 76 can be achieved by the following method and will also give scope for further interesting colour experiments. For the walls you will need some magnolia emulsion as a base and two tubes of gouache (obtainable at an art shop) – one of yellow ochre and one of raw sienna. Use a 1in (25mm) brush – preferably an old, much used one, as it needs to be reasonably stiff to create the effect of a rough, uneven finish. You will also need some small pieces of cotton rag and a small can of matt varnish.

First apply a base coat of magnolia emulsion, also painting a 'test card' with magnolia. When it is thoroughly dry you can begin painting with the gouache mix. Do not be alarmed at the thought of using gouache if this is your first attempt, as it has an advantage over many other paints: if you do not like the effect you can wash it off easily and start again. To mix, squeeze a little yellow ochre and a dash of raw sienna into about ½ pint (0.28l) of magnolia emulsion thinned with a little water, and stir well. Test on the magnolia card until you have a shade you like.

Brush the mixture rapidly on to the house exterior and rub some of it off straight away with a dry rag to achieve a smudged effect. Start at the back of the house for practice and to gain confidence in using this technique. If your first choice of colour is not exactly what you want, wash it off and alter your colour mix. A stone house façade always shows variations in the random colour of the stone, and this method is very satisfactory on a dolls' house.

A similar paint effect can be used on the roof to represent the gentle shades of stone tiles. Use the same base coat and a mix of a greenish khaki and a light brown gouache with the emulsion.

To finish both walls and roof apply a coat of matt varnish, which will seal the surface and keep it clean. The varnish will also darken the paint a little and make it look more mellow.

ROOFS

How to finish a roof is very much a matter of personal preference. A dolls' house is not an architectural model, and two coats of slate grey or terracotta paint followed by one of matt varnish is both easy and elegant.

If you want more realism you may wish to add slates or tiles. Thin wood tiles can be bought in different styles – square, cottagey or pantile – and glued on. Start at the bottom, overlapping each row by about ¼in (6mm), staggering the tiles so that there is a half tile at the end on alternate rows.

Paint the tiled roof with acrylic paint: a mixture of red, brown and yellow will make a warm red-brown; green, grey and yellow will make a good 'grey' slate. Make a shade card before you start painting the roof, so that if you have not mixed enough it will be easy to match the shade later. Some slates here and there should be overpainted in a slightly darker or lighter shade. Finish with a coat of matt varnish.

Realistic looking tiles are also available in plastic fibre which needs no painting. For American-style wooden homes, ready-cut shingles are a good choice. It is best to stain these with wood dye before fixing, and slight

A STEEPLY PITCHED TILED ROOF WITH ATTRACTIVE VARIATIONS IN THE COLOURING ON A NINETEENTH-CENTURY COTTAGE. THIS DELIGHTFUL DOLLS' HOUSE IS A SIMILAR DESIGN TO THE THATCHED COTTAGE (SEE PAGE 99), BUT THE MAKER HAS UPDATED IT TO THE NINETEENTH CENTURY, REPLACING THE THATCH WITH THE TILED ROOF AND ADDING THREE DORMERS, AS MIGHT HAVE BEEN DONE DURING A REBUILDING CONVERSION. IT RETAINS THE LONG SLOPING BACK.

PHOTO COURTESY OF GORDON ROSSITER.

LIGHTWEIGHT AND REALISTIC READY-MADE TILES.

variations in colour will add realism. Home-made tiles can be made by cutting strips of card about $^3/_4$in (19mm) wide and nicking them along the edge to within $^1/_4$in (6mm) of the top. Glue in place with overlaps and finish as described above.

Roof ridging and barge boarding are neat ways to finish a roof and can be chosen to complement the period style of a house. Ready-cut roof ridging can be bought in strips, and metal ridging can be painted white to add a delicate finish to a Regency house. Barge boarding was a feature of Victorian houses and looks very attractive on gable ends.

CHIMNEYS

If your house does not have a chimney, you may want to add one for realism. Ceramic pots and stacks are available to fit most dolls' house roofs, and wooden chimney stacks are available as kits. For a really special chimney to suit, say, a Tudor house, you may need to have one made specially to fit the angle of the roof.

CLUSTERS OF TALL CHIMNEY STACKS WERE A FEATURE OF THE GRAND TUDOR PALACE, SOMETIMES USING BRICKWORK IN CURVING DIAPER PATTERNS TO GOOD EFFECT. THIS SPLENDID CHIMNEY MADE IN WOOD WAS COPIED FROM A TUDOR ORIGINAL BY GORDON ROSSITER TO COMPLETE A SMALL MANOR HOUSE.

INTERIOR

Careful planning of each structural and architectural interior feature is essential if your decoration and furnishings are to show to their best advantage.

STAIRCASE

Unless it is very small, a dolls' house usually has a staircase. Exceptions are some original Victorian houses and commercially made houses of the early twentieth century. In a specially commissioned house the staircase will be complete with balusters, handrail and newel posts; with a less expensive house there might be a simple flight of nicely finished stairs with nosings but without balusters, and in this case you will have to put them in yourself.

Newel posts and balusters in different scales are available in packets of a dozen or so, and handrails are supplied with the groove to take them ready cut. It is better to paint, varnish or stain both the stair treads and fittings before they are fixed together, so that glue does not get on to the bare wood and spoil it.

Cut the top and bottom newel posts to the height desired and glue them in place first, using a general-purpose household adhesive. Leave to set firm for about eight hours before cutting the handrail to size, cutting each end at an angle and gluing it between the posts. Finally, fit each baluster by cutting the top at an angle to fit the grooved rail, and glue in place. Do not be tempted to check whether it is firm while the glue is setting, as full strength is not reached for several hours and you could dislodge it. Completing a staircase is straightforward providing you follow this sequence.

MAKING A STAIRCASE

If no staircase is fitted and the floors are not yet fixed in place, you can cut out a stairwell and install a staircase; ready-made ones can be bought to fit standard room heights. An alternative is to make your own using triangular wood strip, which is available from DIY stores in two sizes, ^{1}/2in (13mm) or ^{3}/4in (19mm). This will make the rise the same size as the tread for each step and the angle (45°) much steeper than in the full-size version. But this is well suited to the dolls' house because in a ^{1}/12-scale house the average room height is 10in–12in (25.4cm–30.5cm) in a room about 12in (30.5cm) deep; stairs with shallower treads would extend out into the street.

To make a staircase you need to cut a piece of thin wood the same width as the stairwell and long enough to fit when placed at 45°. Trim the ends at an angle so that it fits flush at top and bottom. Cut steps the same width from the triangular strip, check that the position of the top step is level with the floor above and space the rest evenly so that the bottom step is the same height as the rest, then glue the steps on to the wooden base. The flight is then ready to be fixed in by gluing to the floor at the bottom, to the edge of the aperture at the top, and against the adjoining side wall. However, once the staircase is made and the fit checked, it is best not to fix it in permanently until after the walls have been decorated.

CHIMNEY BREASTS

The one immovable feature will be the chimney breast. Sometimes these are already provided in a ready-made house, but if they are not it adds realism if they can be properly sited below any chimney on the roof. But dolls' houses do not need to be totally accurate, and if the house is very small it is often preferable to save space and fit a fireplace directly on to the wall.

Fireplaces in bedrooms are not essential, but they add to the cosy feeling in a Victorian or Edwardian house. If you want to include a fireplace in a bedroom it would be realistic to site the chimney breast above the one in the room below, although to save space you might consider a corner fireplace and assume a bend in the flue.

If you plan to fit ready-made fireplaces you need to make your choice first so that you can make the chimney breast the right size. If you make your own fireplaces you can cut the hole for the grate and make the fireplace to fit afterwards. Either way, once the chimney breast is fitted you can delay gluing

IN ORDER TO FIT BOTH A RANGE AND A DRESSER INTO SUCH A SMALL KITCHEN, THE RANGE HAS BEEN SITED ON THE BACK WALL. THE FIREPLACE IN THE BEDROOM ABOVE IS FITTED TO THE SIDE WALL TO ALLOW ENOUGH SPACE FOR A BED. THIS KIND OF DEPARTURE FROM WHAT WOULD BE POSSIBLE IN REALITY IS SOMETIMES NECESSARY IF A PLEASING OVERALL EFFECT IS TO BE ACHIEVED.

IN A SMALL HOUSE A CORNER CHIMNEY BREAST CAN BE A SPACE-SAVING FEATURE.

the fireplace in position permanently until after you have dealt with the flooring.

Choose wood about ¹/₂in (13mm) thick and cut the chimney breast to run from floor to ceiling and a little wider than the fireplace you intend to fit, cutting out a hole to take a grate in the centre. For a Tudor house or cottage where an inglenook fireplace is appropriate, it will need to be about 1in (25mm) deep and can run the entire length of a rear wall.

A wooden chimney breast provides a firm base for miniature bricks if you decide on exposed brickwork, which can be effective in the right setting. If the chimney breast is to be papered over you can use polyboard (available from art shops), which consists of a layer of foam sandwiched between two layers of card. It is light in weight and can be cut with a craft knife with care, as the filling can crumble.

CORNER CHIMNEY BREAST

For a corner chimney breast you need a piece of wood with the edges cut at an angle to fit flush with the walls on either side, and a hole for the grate. Alternatively, you can assume an exterior chimney breast and simply make a triangular wooden shelf to fit across the corner, supporting it with a strip of moulding fitted over the fireplace. This type of deep mantelshelf is ideal for displaying an ornament, perhaps a Chinese vase or Staffordshire china figure.

FIREPLACES

A simple fireplace can be made from one flat piece of wood with a hole cut for the grate. Add a mantelshelf supported by brackets or a strip of moulding; make the brackets by cutting two thin slices of suitable moulding and gluing them about ⅜in (1cm) from each end of the mantelshelf. Use half-round dowelling to make a 'pillar' on either side of the grate. Both pillars and fireplace surround can be painted or covered with marbled paper. Mantelshelf mouldings are available in a selection of styles and sizes.

For something more elaborate you need a few different sizes of small wood mouldings, either specially designed for the purpose or from your local DIY store. Look at some real fireplaces or pictures in a book or magazine as examples, decide which sizes of wood mouldings would be most suitable for your chosen design and arrange them in different ways until you like the effect. The corners of the mouldings need to be mitred to fit together neatly on both fireplace surround and mantelshelf.

A tiled surround will be suitable for many period fireplaces, and you can use either ceramic tiles (*see* pages 79 and 138) or paper with a printed

PHOTO BY IAN KEAREY.

design. In either case check the measurements before making up the fireplace surround so that the tiles fit exactly.

MAKING A FIREPLACE FROM A KIT

Fireplace kits are available in both wood and metal. The wooden ones come with instructions in a variety of period styles, and the finished fireplace will be less expensive than the fully finished ready-made version. Most metal kits are replicas of Victorian cast-iron fireplaces, decorated with ornate swags and garlands. To look authentic these should be painted matt black, but the effect of using white paint can be very pretty in a small room.

An effective instant fireplace can be made by cutting a small picture frame in half and painting it a suitable colour.

GRATE

Glue in a piece of matt black card as a base and line the sides of the grate aperture with black card or paper. You will need to fit a grate of some kind: a fire basket contrived from black card is usually adequate, as once the fire is laid very little can be seen of the base itself.

For a Georgian room you might prefer a metal replica of a period grate. An Adam-style grate is especially attractive, and the surround in front of the fireplace should be of 'marble' with no fender. For a Victorian fireplace you can make a fender from brass filigree strip, which is available from model shops, or cut a thin old gilt bracelet to size.

LAYING THE FIRE

Use a sliver of wood covered with black paper or painted matt black as a base for the fire. Build up layers of either small twigs or railway modeller's 'coal', together with a little strategically placed shiny red transparent paper. Glue each layer into place separately, dab with glue and sprinkle with red glitter.

For a summery effect place a paper fan or a flower arrangement or vase in the grate instead of a fire.

FLOORING

There is a wide choice of dolls' house flooring to suit any period. If the wood used to make the house is of sufficiently good quality you can sand, stain and polish the existing floor, adding rugs when the rest of the decorations are complete. In most cases, however, you will want to fit additional flooring, and whatever you choose will work best if you make a pattern for the floor of each room from thin, good quality card. Mark the front edge and which room it is for on the reverse of your card template in order to avoid any mistakes at a later stage. You can then fix the chosen flooring on to this card and glue the entire false floor into the house in one piece.

FLAGSTONES AND WIDE OAK PLANKING IN ADJOINING ROOMS OF A TUDOR HOUSE. THE FLAGSTONES PROVIDED BY TERRY CURRAN HAVE BEEN GRIMED TO SIMULATE THE CONDITIONS IN A SIXTEENTH-CENTURY KITCHEN.

PLANKED FLOORING

Planked flooring using strips of 'iron-on' veneer will be suitable for most period houses. In Tudor and Georgian houses the floorboards were wider than those used today, and in $1/12$ scale $3/4$in (19mm) looks about right; $1/2$in (13mm) width would be more suitable for a later house. Suit the wood to the period – oak for Tudor, mahogany for Georgian and Regency, pine for Victorian.

Use a flat piece of wood as an ironing board. Cut the planks to suitable lengths, with some variation so they can be staggered. In a real house the joists usually run across and the floorboards run from front to back of the house, but it will look better in a dolls' house if you have the floorboards crosswise so that the front edge is straight.

Begin at the front with one long board across the complete width of the room for neatness. After you iron each plank on to the card, push the strips together and press down firmly with a small block of wood, as the action of lifting the iron away can pull the strips apart. Try the false floor for size and trim away any excess at the back and sides. Stain and polish the floor before fitting it in place.

PARQUET FLOOR

Iron-on planking is adaptable and can be used to lay a parquet floor by cutting the strips to a length of about $1^{1}/_{4}$in (32mm) and arranging them in the familiar zigzag design (*see* page 65). This is not difficult, but it is time-consuming. For accuracy make a card template of the size required and mark the planks on the reverse before cutting. A parquet floor will look best if the zigzag pattern is cut straight along each edge and framed with a border of four straight planks, each the length of a whole edge of the floor with the corners mitred to make a frame.

TILED FLOOR

Black and white iron-on floor tiles of plasticized card can be applied to a base card to make an effective hall or kitchen floor (*see* page 63). Ceramic quarry tiles or flagstones can be glued on using fabric glue. Both can be cut to fit the space available if you follow the maker's instructions. To make a lino floor for a 1930s kitchen, use one full-size vinyl floor tile of a suitable design. A cork tablemat cut into 1in (25mm) squares will make a floor for a bathroom.

THE STAIR CARPET MADE FROM FURNISHING BRAID IS READY TO BE LAID IN THIS REGENCY HOUSE.

FITTED CARPETS

You might want to have fitted carpets in a modern house. Fine woollen dress material is excellent for this purpose, and can be plain or textured; thin velvet or fine needlecord are also suitable. Carpet can be cut to size, glued to a card base and, unlike other floor materials, fixed in *after* the painting and wallpapering are finished and the skirting boards put in, to avoid marking the fabric with paint or glue, as a single mark on fabric is disastrous.

STAIR CARPET

It is easier to carpet stairs before you fix the staircase permanently in place. Furnishing braid makes excellent stair carpet: there are so many widths and patterns available that you will be able to find one to suit any style of decoration (*see* pages 54 and 113). Use a strip of double-sided tape down the stairs to hold the carpet in place. Scaled-down woven carpet from Turkey, thin enough to bend round the edges of the stairs easily, is a more expensive but exquisite option.

FRONT DOOR

The front door is often the first thing you notice about a house. It can make or mar the façade, so it is worth taking trouble when choosing the paint colour and the door furniture (*see* page 49). If you are restoring an old home-made house it will probably be worth replacing the door with something more appropriate to your chosen style. A new door frame, perhaps surmounted by a canopy or surrounded by a built-on porch, can often improve a plain door out of all recognition.

PHOTO COURTESY OF MULVANY & ROGERS.

The front door of a dolls' house will be enhanced by the addition of suitable door furniture. For a Tudor house, black 'iron' fittings on a planked door will be best. Brass latch hooks are available and can be painted matt black using model paint. Strap hinges are not easy to find; draw and make a template and cut them out in card which can then be painted matt black to match the handle.

Brass door furniture is suitable for later periods, and there are various styles available which can be glued on. When attaching handles or doorknobs with a small pin at the back, you will need to drill a hole in the door. Put a dab of glue on the backplate before pushing the pin firmly into the hole.

INTERNAL DOORS

Internal doors are an optional feature in a dolls' house. A simple arched opening between rooms is often considered sufficient (*see* page 150) and provides a feeling of space; however, some houses need doors. If you want to provide doors and the doorways are of a suitable size, kits are available for you to assemble a four- or six-panel door in mahogany or jelutong (a softer wood which takes stain well), constructed by the same method as a full-size door, and the finished item will be extremely attractive.

PHOTO COURTESY OF GORDON ROSSITER.

DOORS FITTED TO THE BACK WALL OF A SIMPLE THREE-STOREY DOLLS' HOUSE GIVE AN IMPRESSION THAT THERE ARE FURTHER ROOMS AT THE BACK.

Fixing brings its own problems: most dolls' house stockists will offer helpful advice, but it is not easy to deal with the minute screws supplied for tiny hinges; you will need a small drill and special tweezers with an attached magnifying glass to do this successfully. In most cases it is satisfactory to omit the screws and simply glue on the hinges; many professional dolls' house makers choose this method. Needless to say, this needs a strong glue.

If you want to make internal doors yourself, remember to allow sufficient clearance for any flooring or carpet which may be fitted later – do some advance planning in this respect. A plain wooden door can look very attractive in certain room settings if it is papered or covered with material to match the decor – perhaps to make a 'jib' door in a Georgian room or a 'secret' door in a Queen Anne library. This is also a suitable simple treatment for the inside of a plain front door. For a Tudor house or cottage you need a planked door with a Z-frame. This is simple to make from stripwood, with the Z-frame glued on afterwards (see page 100).

In most rooms of later eras you will want to fit a panelled door; it is never satisfactory just to cut wooden door panels and glue them on to the face of the door – the result invariably looks amateurish and slightly crooked. A better method is to use some iron-on planking cut to suitable widths and to add the rails and stiles, leaving part of the door base exposed to form the panels. For complete realism very fine beading with the corners mitred can be used to edge the panels. The door should be finely sanded and then painted to obtain a good finish. Stain or varnish is unlikely to give a satisfactory appearance, as the different woods used will take the colour differently.

DOOR CASINGS

Make a door casing from three pieces of wood moulding mitred at the corners. Paint the mouldings before assembly and glue round the door after completing the wallpapering, to cover the edges. Doors were an imposing feature of Georgian rooms, and a simple doorcase can be made more elaborate by the addition of a pediment or additional moulding over the door.

WINDOWS

Many dolls' houses are supplied without window glazing, ready for you to fit your own after painting the exterior. Various standard sizes of windows are available in acetate screenprinted with white window bars. These should be fixed to the inside of the house, and need to be slightly oversize so that they can overlap all round the window aperture by about 1/4in (6mm). The edges can then be covered with a window frame made from suitable wooden mouldings.

FITTING WINDOW GLAZING

Use an orange stick to apply a very small amount of general-purpose glue on to the wall around the window aperture; leave for a few seconds to become tacky

and then press the glazing gently into place. This method will avoid the possibility of the glue leaving an unsightly trail across the clean surface of the glazing.

If the house is fitted with wooden glazing bars you can cut windows from plain acetate sheet (available from model shops) with scissors and fix them in the same way.

LATTICE OR DIAMOND-PANED WINDOWS

This type of window – for a Tudor house, a cottage or a 1920s or 1930s house – can be reproduced in rigid wire mesh with the glazing fixed behind, but really needs the expertise of a metalworker to achieve a successful result. As an alternative you can rule the lattice out on acetate using a black overhead

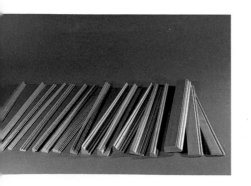

projection pen from an art shop. This is normally used for writing on the transparencies of overhead projectors and can produce exactly the right thickness of line without difficulty.

GOTHICK WINDOWS

In Gothick (*see* page 51) the windows, as in the original Gothic, define the style and can be made very easily by cutting a paper pattern the same size as your dolls' house window and marking in pointed arch shapes between the upright glazing bars. Cut the shape out on white card and fix it in behind the top of the existing window with a very little glue around the outside edge. Gothick windows are not easy to curtain, and look best when outlined with thin braid.

WINDOW FRAMES

Window frames are made in the same way as door casings (*see* page 143). In practice it is often unnecessary to provide a complete internal window frame, as the top and sides of the window fixing will be hidden behind a pelmet and curtains (*see* page 146). If this is the case, all you need is a small strip of wood to provide a windowsill; check that this will not come between the edge of a floor and the opening front of the house and prevent the front closing.

SKIRTING BOARDS, CORNICES, DADO RAILS AND PICTURE RAILS

It is always worth fitting skirting boards and cornices to make a neat edge; they also serve a useful purpose, concealing any slight irregularity or gap around the edges of floor covering or wallpaper. It is important to choose the correctly detailed shapes for the period of the house. Scaled-down replicas of period styles are available in 12in (30.5cm) or 18in (45.7cm) lengths and can be cut to fit, so the first step is to take measurements and work out how much you need, allowing the extra length required to mitre the corners. It is also worth buying an extra piece of matching moulding for any alterations.

HOW TO FIT

Cut the skirting board and cornice for the rear wall first, then the sides, and check the fit. Label each piece on the reverse in pencil, identifying which room it is intended for and whether for back, left or right. Dado rails for the Georgian room and picture rails for rooms of later perods should also be cut and labelled and have the fit checked at this stage.

Paint or varnish these fittings and lay them aside until the rest of the decorations are completed.

THERE IS A WIDE VARIETY OF WOODEN MOULDINGS AVAILABLE FOR THE DOLLS' HOUSE DECORATOR.

THE WALLPAPER IN THESE ROOMS
CREATES A COOL, ELEGANT
EFFECT.

WITH THE DOORS AT THE FRONT OF
THE HOUSE OPEN, THE UNOBTRU-
SIVE WALLPAPER IS A PERFECT
SETTING FOR THE RICHLY
COLOURED CURTAINS.

WALLPAPER

You now have a dolls' house complete with its internal fixtures – doors, flooring, chimney breasts and fireplaces – plus several prepared fittings ready to be put in after you have finished decorating; it is now time to plan your colour schemes, bearing in mind the probable tastes of the inhabitants.

Dolls' house wallpaper comes in a great variety of tiny patterns and colours, so it should be easy to find some that you like, taking into account the chosen flooring and general style of the rooms. Do not neglect the possibilities of giftwrapping paper: some designs are ideal for use as wallpaper, and a large sheet is inexpensive. In general, pastel colours are preferable, as it is important to make the interior as light as possible – a strong colour can look over-emphatic in a small room.

Most British dolls' houses open at the front with one or two large doors, and it looks better, because it is more restful, if the full width of the inside of the opening wall is covered with a single design rather than matching each of the adjacent rooms (see page 115). Choose the least obtrusive design used. If the house is very large and has a separate opening for each storey, the inside can be painted or papered to match the facing rooms on each floor without looking fussy.

Measure the rooms carefully before you shop for paper, allowing for any repeat pattern and making sure you have enough. It is not necessary for the

paper to fit exactly at ceiling and floor, as the edges will be covered when you fit skirting boards and cornices. It is a good idea to buy extra paper in case of mistakes or to keep for future repair or restoration.

Applying wallpaper in a dolls' house is simple: make a paper pattern the exact size of each wall and cut the wallpaper fractionally larger to allow for a small overlap in the back corners. Use ordinary wallpaper paste mixed a little thinner than usual, and size the walls the day before wallpapering.

SPECIAL PAINT FINISHES AND SIMULATED EFFECTS

Dragging, sponging, combing, marbling, stippling and stencilling have all become familiar to the do-it-yourself decorator, and a wealth of information has been published explaining how to produce these effects.

IT TOOK A YEAR'S WORK FOR MULVANY & ROGERS TO COMPLETE THEIR MINIATURE VERSION OF THE PALACE OF VERSAILLES. AS IN THE REAL PALACE, THE SHEER MAGNIFICENCE OF THE DECOR-ATIONS AND FURNISHINGS IS BREATHTAKING. IT IS NOW IN THE ANGELS ATTIC MUSEUM IN CALIFORNIA, HELPING TO RAISE MONEY FOR AUTISTIC CHILDREN.

PHOTO COURTESY OF MULVANY & ROGERS.

While in theory most of these specialized finishes would be equally suitable in the dolls' house, the application of these techniques is limited because of the very small areas to be decorated. When you are dealing with skirting board which is only $\frac{1}{2}$in (13mm) high and a wall which measures perhaps 10in x 7in (25.4cm x 17.8cm), such treatments do not produce an effect in proportion to the effort expended by a non-professional. The widely available wood tone varnishes in a variety of unusual colours, e.g. blue spruce, peachwood, silver birch or sage, will be just as effective as laborious hand graining when applied to an architrave or surround which is only $\frac{3}{8}$in (10mm) wide.

PHOTO COURTESY OF CHARLOTTE HUNT MINIATURES.

THE WALL PANELS IN THIS EXQUISITE ROOM SETTING ARE BASED ON THOSE IN A SWEDISH MANOR HOUSE IN THE GUSTAVIAN STYLE. BOTH PANELS AND STOVE WERE HAND-PAINTED BY CHARLOTTE HUNT. THE GILDED CHAIRS ARE IN THE STYLE OF LOUIS XVI, SHOWING THE STRONG FRENCH INFLUENCE ON SWEDISH INTERIORS IN THE EIGHTEENTH CENTURY.

STENCILLING

One old technique which has regained popularity is stencilling, which is extremely useful for decorating walls, floors and furniture, just as it is in the full-size house. However, for stencilling on walls, because of the difficulty of reaching into the back of a dolls' house room, it is often easier to cut a paper pattern of the walls, using stiff paper or thin card to make a template. Colourwash some good quality lining paper, and when it is thoroughly dry use your template to cut out a pattern of the three walls of the room in one long strip, leaving a little extra at the ends for final fitting adjustment. Stencil your design on to the paper, and when it is completed paste in your finished walls without any need for joining at the corners. When the paste has thoroughly dried out cut off any excess at the front edges with a craft knife or scalpel.

When colouring very small stencils you need to use a tiny brush rather than even the smallest stencilling brush. A useful alternative for miniaturists is to use waterproof coloured pencils, which are available in a wide range of pastel colours from art shops.

SIMULATED EFFECTS

Painted wall panelling is an attractive feature which can be achieved even if you have no skill as an artist. The preparation may take a little time, as you need to collect small pictures from magazines or greetings cards. For Tudor-style wall panelling you could concentrate on flower paintings or botanical prints. For a house of a later period tiled pictures set into panels give a clean, fresh effect in kitchen or dairy. In a Georgian room precious wallpaper was often set into moulded panels if it was too expensive to cover all the walls of a room.

TROMPE L'OEIL

One of the guiding principles in interior design is that if the space is not there, it can be achieved visually. The basic dolls' house, consisting of a box divided into four rooms with a central walled-in staircase, can feel sadly cramped. This kind of staircase can be made to look less like a tunnel by using light wallpaper and stair carpet. It may also help to hang a mirror at the top of the stairs; if the landing is wide enough, the mirror can be positioned to give a reflection into one of the adjoining rooms. If this is not possible, try to fit in a pillar or statue or fix a bracket support on the wall to hold a vase or ornament so that it is reflected in the glass.

THE GREETINGS CARD USED AS A FAKE VIEW THROUGH A DOORWAY INCLUDED THE PERSPECTIVE EFFECT OF A BLUE-AND-WHITE TILED FLOOR. THE ILLUSION WAS INCREASED BY PUTTING A STEP AND WOODEN DOOR SURROUND IN FRONT OF THE CARD.

CAREFULLY POSITIONING HOUSE-
HOLD PARAPHERNALIA – IN THIS
CASE A SEA CAPTAIN'S BASKET
AND CATCH – CAN HELP TO
DISGUISE THE BORDER BETWEEN
FLOOR AND PAINTING.

Another way to create space is to give an impression of further rooms out of sight. Fake doors and staircases which disappear behind walls are useful ways of extending the space at your disposal. Put a door at the back of a room, fixing it flat against the wall, and fit a doorcasing around it: the room will appear larger (*see* pages 93 and 142).

Stairs which disappear behind an archway also add a feeling of extra rooms beyond. You need only fit three or four stair treads leading off behind an extra false wall fitted into the back of the house. An effective way to arrange this is to cut a piece of plywood or thick card the same size as the back wall and cut out an archway.

Fit the extra wall in front of the 'stairs'. You will lose a little actual room space – the same measurement as the width of the stair treads – but the visual trick makes the room appear larger. There will be slightly less space to display furniture, so this arrangement works best in an entrance hall rather than leading off a main room.

A fake window or glass-panelled doorway at the back of a house can be equally effective in showing some of the 'garden' beyond. You need to find a suitable picture to put in behind an acetate window: a greetings card showing a garden scene will be in the right scale. The optical illusion is reinforced by fitting a window frame and a small interior windowsill to hold a plant in a pot (*see* page 86).

SOFT FURNISHINGS

When the decorations are finished you can enjoy making curtains and other soft furnishings. Lacy curtains or festoon blinds, side curtains with tie-backs of thin gold cord or narrow ribbon, tailored pelmets or roller blinds are all much easier to make in the miniature scale than full-size. The only problem will be in finding materials that are delicate enough. Fine cotton lawn or Indian silk are ideal, as they are not too stiff to arrange in graceful folds. Synthetic materials are never satisfactory, as they will not stay put.

THE DELICATE PASTEL COLOURS OF THE CURTAINS ADD THE PERFECT FINISHING TOUCH TO A ¹/₁₆-SCALE REGENCY HOUSE.

CURTAINS

To avoid extra bulk, omit the hems altogether and wipe along the edges with a miniscule amount of fabric glue to prevent fraying. Gather or pleat the top of the curtain by hand and attach it to a piece of narrow tape a little wider than the window. The curtains can then be glued directly on to the wall and the tape covered by a pelmet or a strip of braid.

For a period house you may prefer to hang curtains from a curtain pole. Brass or wooden poles are available in various lengths which can be cut down to fit your windows, and tiny curtain rings are supplied. To make your own pole, use some thin dowelling, or a wooden cocktail stick for a very small window. Add two small beads to make finials on either end; the curtains can be hung from gilt jump rings intended for jewellery making.

PELMETS

All sorts of fancy shapes can be made with ease from a few scraps of leftover curtain material or from braid or lace edging. Haberdashery departments of large stores stock a large range of suitable braids and lace trimmings, and packets of miniscule made-up ribbon bows and silk flowers intended as dress trimmings can be used to add a finishing touch to many period curtain arrangements.

Drape and gather the pelmet material or lace so that it extends just beyond the outer edges of the curtains. A simple, straight pelmet can be made from a strip of braid which tones with the curtain fabric. You can also make a more rigid, shaped pelmet from thin card covered with fabric, and this can be scalloped, curved or castellated. Draw half your pattern on to folded paper to ensure symmetry before cutting out on card. Glue the fabric lightly on to the card and trim the edges when the glue is dry. You will need fabric on both sides of the card if the back of the pelmet will be visible from outside the window. Trim with a bobble fringe or a strip of very fine braid.

BLINDS

Blinds are a neat and attractive alternative to curtains if you want all the windows to match from outside the house. Plain roller blinds are simple to make and are suitable for the kitchen of a modern house or the servant's quarters in a period house. For a non-working roller blind you need a piece of thin round dowelling about $1/2$in (13mm) wider than the window and sharpened at both ends, or a cocktail stick if the length is suitable. Glue a small washer and a bead on to each end.

Cut a piece of material a little longer than the length you want to have the finished blind and the exact width to fit between the washers on the dowelling. Roll it once round the dowelling and glue in place. To finish the blind add a strip of lace to the bottom and attach a short length of silk cord with a tiny bead glued or sewn on to the end as a pull cord.

Festoon blinds are enjoying a new wave of popularity with today's home owners, but they were also in use in Georgian homes. For a ruched festoon blind you will need a piece of very thin material about double the width of the window and about three-quarters of the length. Fold in half lengthwise, sew the side seams, turn and press. Make two rows of gathers at equal intervals, pull up to form ruches and knot the thread firmly. Glue the finished blind on to a thin strip of card and glue just above the window.

MATERIAL EFFECTS

Curtains need not be limited to windows: in the Longleat dolls' house of 1870 the entire back wall of the drawing room is curtained with pleated silk, which gives it a sumptuous effect. The material should be gathered very neatly and can be glued directly on to the wall at the top and the edge covered in thin braid. In a modern house a fine cotton fabric with a very small design would give the effect of curtains drawn at night over an invisible rear window.

BED HANGINGS

A curtained hanging suspended from a gilded circlet over a bed looks very luxurious. You need a small section of cardboard tube as a base for the top; one from the inside of a packet of food wrap is suitable. Cut it about $^1/_2$in (13mm) deep and paint it gold. Cover with braid and glue two lengths of gathered material inside, long enough to reach the floor when draped on either side of the bed. Glue the tube to the ceiling and arrange the folds carefully, fastening them with a tie-back on either side of the bed, use an old pair of earrings instead of a material tie-back.

HANDMADE RUGS

If you have decided on having beautifully polished floors you may want to add some rugs. The traditional way of making a dolls' house rug is in fine needlepoint, and if you enjoy needlework you can use this method and suit the colours to the room decorations.

THE RUG IN THIS VICTORIAN BEDROOM COMPLEMENTS THE COLOURS OF THE BEDSPREAD AND WALLPAPER.

EXAMPLES OF NEEDLEPOINT WORKED ON DIFFERENT BACKINGS BY GILLIAN EARL, WHO SPECIALIZES IN MINIATURE NEEDLEPOINT CUSHIONS AND CARPETS.

Canvas with 18 holes to the inch (25mm) and one strand of Persian yarn or two threads of crewel wool would be suitable for a $^1/_{12}$-scale house. If you are experienced and your eyesight is good you may want to consider something even finer, worked in silk on canvas with up to 48 holes to the inch. Designs for dolls' house rugs are available as charts or complete kits from several suppliers, in a variety of patterns to suit different room styles from sixteenth-century to modern.

You can also design your own rug to fit an exact size. This is straightforward if you plan your design on graph paper to make your own chart, remembering one square on the paper equals one thread on the canvas. It is only necessary to plot half of a symmetrical design; and when working, remember not to duplicate the centre row of stitches.

A piece of woollen fabric can be used as an alternative to a worked carpet. Tweedy, textured fabrics with a fleck or variations in colour look attractive in a modern setting. If you are able to obtain them, manufacturer's sample squares are useful for this purpose, as the edges are already whipped.

For the Victorian house you can use a circular table mat, some of which, made from a velvety material embroidered with coloured threads and with braided edges, make convincing carpets; these are widely available in linen departments. Oriental silk mats are another possibility where a Chinese carpet would be suitable, and these are also made in several sizes.

For the old-fashioned kitchen you might like to have a traditional rag rug; this is not difficult to make, but it does need time and patience. You will need a piece of tarlatan, which is available in both black and white, suitable for a dark or pastel rug. Cut lengths of thin fabric into ¼in (6mm) wide strips. Weave the strips in and out of the mesh with a darning needle; do not pull tight, but leave loops on top. Use colours at random, with a good mixture of different shades. When all the mesh has been filled, trim the loops, rub your hand gently over the surface of the rug and give it a little shake to fluff up the 'rags'.

PHOTO COURTESY OF CAROL BLACK MINIATURES.

FURNITURE

Choosing the miniature furniture for your house will be a gradual process. It is not always possible to furnish entirely with craftsman-made pieces, and you may enjoy adding to the furnishings by making some of your own. Unless you are an experienced cabinetmaker or have taken a specialized woodworking course, you are unlikely to be able to make miniature furniture that will stand comparison with pieces made by experienced craftspeople. However, many specialists now produce furniture in kit form, and kits are ideal for someone with no carpentry skills who would still like to make up their own dolls' house furniture. If the instructions are followed carefully and enough time is allowed, the resulting piece will be a pleasure to the owner.

THIS WELL-CONSTRUCTED WOODEN DRESSER KIT FROM BARBARA ANNE MINIATURES COMES WITH CLEAR INSTRUCTIONS AND WOULD LOOK GOOD STAINED OR VARNISHED (SEE PAGE 91), OR PAINTED IN IMITATION OF STENCILLED FURNITURE.

Assembling furniture from kits is also a good way to learn how miniature pieces are constructed, the most suitable types of wood and the joints used, perhaps with a view to going on and making furniture yourself when you have gained experience in this way. One point to watch is the finish: many beautifully made pieces are spoiled by too high a polish or too thick a coat of paint, and it is worth taking a great deal of trouble with rubbing down between coats of varnish or paint, or learning how to French polish.

FINISHING TOUCHES

There are many everyday objects which you can adapt to make useful accessories to give character to your dolls' house.

✤ Unusual beads make good vases – macrame beads are especially good for this purpose.
✤ An elegant silver fruit bowl can be made by using two different sizes of dome-shaped filigree jewellery mounts glued together so that the smaller one forms the base.
✤ Small glass ornaments can be used as bookends.
✤ Toggles and plain beads make good light shades for a modern house.
✤ A toothpaste tube cap covered in fabric, with the inside painted and half-filled with a few bits of screwed-up paper, will make a wastepaper bin.
✤ A small perfume bottle can be used as a lamp base, with a shade made from a cone of paper edged with a fine braid.
✤ The harmless broken windscreen glass which is all too often found on street corners will represent crushed ice around miniature bottles of wine or champagne in an ice bucket.

❖ Fruit can be shaped from modelling compound and painted. With a little practice you will be able to make mouth-wateringly realistic food for the kitchen or dining table. The best for this purpose is modelling compound which can be hardened in the oven (it takes about 20 minutes at a temperature of 212°–275°F or 100°–135°C) to make your modelled food permanent. The compound comes in a wide range of colours, or you can use neutral and paint it yourself. Make sure that miniature food does not get into the hands of small children who could choke if they mistook it for something edible.

❖ Make towels from ordinary white tape; fringe the ends by pulling the threads across and draw stripes with a red or blue ballpoint pen.

FRUIT IN A BOWL AND FLOWERS IN A POT.

REALISTIC TOWELS OF DIFFERENT STYLES AIRING ON A MINIATURE CLOTHES RAIL.

❖ Knit a bathmat in crochet cotton and embroider 'BATH' on it in blue stranded cotton.

❖ Make a bell pull with very narrow embroidered ribbon and finish the end by mitring the corners and attaching a small bead or bell.

❖ Make cushions from satin ribbon stuffed with a twist of synthetic filling – be careful not to overstuff.

❖ Leave some miniature knitting around to add a lived-in look. You need a small round bead with a large centre hole, very fine darning or tapestry wool, and some shirt pins with fancy heads. To make a neat 'ball of wool', thread a length of wool on to a fine needle and work round the bead until it is covered and the centre hole is full. With good eyesight or the aid of a magnifier you can knit two or three rows on the shirt pins – six stitches is enough. You can also buy needles of carved bone, but these are naturally very fragile, so it is best to do the actual knitting on pins and transfer the finished work to the bone needles.

FURTHER
INFORMATION

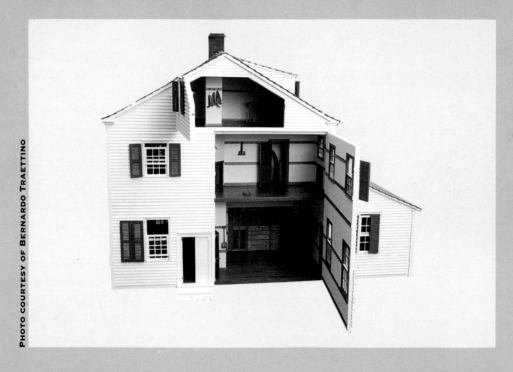

BIBLIOGRAPHY

Agius, Pauline, *Ackermann's Regency Furniture and Interiors,* The Crowood Press, 1984

Anscombe, Isabelle, *Arts and Crafts Style*, Phaidon (Oxford), 1991

Aslin, Elizabeth, *E.W.Godwin Furniture and Interior Decoration*, John Murray, 1988

Beard, Geoffrey, *The Work of Robert Adam*, John Bartholomew, 1978

Benson, E.F., *Mapp and Lucia*, William Heinemann

Brunskill, Ronald and **Clifton-Taylor**, Alec, *English Brickwork*, Ward Lock, 1977

Chambers, James, *The English House*, Methuen, 1985

Clifton-Taylor, Alec, *The Pattern of English Building*, Faber & Faber, 1972

Collard, Frances, *Regency Furniture*, Antique Collectors' Club, 1985

Cornforth, John, *The Search for a Style: Country Life and Architecture 1897–1935*, André Deutsch, 1988

Davidson, Caroline, *The World of Mary Ellen Best*, Chatto & Windus, 1985

Fletcher, Ronald, *The Parkers at Saltram 1769–89*, British Broadcasting Corporation, 1970

Girouard, Mark, *The Victorian Country House*, Yale University Press, 1979

Glasgow School of Art, *Charles Rennie Mackintosh*, Richard Drew, 1987

Gooden, Susanna, *A History of Heal's*, Heal and Son, 1984

Greene, Vivien, *English Dolls' Houses*, Bell & Hyman, 1955

Greene, Vivien, *Family Dolls' Houses*, G.Bell and Sons, 1973

Hackney, Fiona and Isla, *Charles Rennie Mackintosh*, Quintet, 1989

Harris, Nathaniel, *Chippendale*, Octopus, 1989

Haslam, Malcolm, *Arts and Crafts Carpets*, David Black Oriental Carpets, 1991

Hayward, Helena (ed.), *World Furniture*, Paul Hamlyn, 1965

Heal, Sir Ambrose, *London Furniture Makers 1660–1840*, Batsford, 1953

Heron, Marianne, *In the Houses of Ireland*, Thames and Hudson, 1988 (Stewart, Tabori and Chang Inc., USA)

Hicks, David, *Style and Design*, Viking, 1987 (Little, Brown and Company, Canada)

Jackson, Valerie, *Dolls' Houses and Miniatures*, John Murray, 1988

Lasdun, Susan, *Victorians at Home*, Weidenfeld & Nicholson, 1981

Lyall, Sutherland, *Dream Cottages*, Robert Hale, 1988

MacQuoid, Percy, *A History of English Furniture*, Bracken Books, 1988

Marshall, John and **Willox**, Ian, *The Victorian House*, Sidgwick & Jackson, 1981

Milhofer, Stefan A., *Oriental Rugs*, Phaidon, 1976

Morris, William, *William Morris by Himself*, Macdonald, 1988

Mungay, Gordon, *Miss Hurst Dancing and Other Scenes from Regency Life 1812–1823*, Victor Gollancz, 1981

Osband, Linda, *Victorian House Style*, David & Charles, 1991

Priestley, J.B., *The Prince of Pleasure and His Regency 1811–20*, William Heinemann, 1969

Prizeman, John, *Your House, the Outside View*, Quiller Press, 1975

Reid, Richard, *The Georgian House and Its Details*, Bishopsgate Press, 1988

Sheraton Furniture Designs from 'The Cabinet-Maker's Book' 1791– 94, John Tiranti, 1946

Swindells, David, *Restoring Period Timber-Framed Houses*, David & Charles, 1987

Sykes, Christopher Simon, *Ancient English Houses*, Chatto & Windus, 1988

Symonds, R.W. and **Whineray**, B.B., *Victorian Furniture*, Studio Editions, 1987

Watkinson, Ray, *William Morris as Designer*, Studio Vista, 1967

Woodforde, John, *Georgian Houses for All*, Routledge & Kegan Paul, 1978

FURTHER PRACTICAL READING

DOLLS' HOUSES

Cole, Christopher, *Make Your Own Dolls' House*, David & Charles, 1990

Morse, Michal, *Build a Dolls' House*, Batsford, 1992

Nickolls, Brian, *Making Dolls' Houses in 1/12 Scale*, David & Charles, 1991

Rowbottom, Derek, *Making Tudor Dolls' Houses*, GMC Publications, 1990

Rowbottom, Derek, *Making Georgian Dolls' Houses*, GMC Publications, 1992

FURNITURE

Davenport, John, *Making Miniature Furniture*, Batsford, 1988

Spalding, Graham, *Making Unusual Miniatures*, GMC Publications, 1989

DOLLS

Atkinson, Sue, *Making and Dressing Dolls' House Dolls*, David & Charles, 1992

FURNISHINGS

Brown, Jean, *Embroidery in Miniature*, Batsford, 1987

Folk, Eileen, *Needlework Designs for Miniature Projects*, Dover Publications (New York), 1984

McBaine, Susan, *Miniature Needlepoint Rugs for Dollhouses*, Dover Publications (New York), 1976

Sorensen, Grethe, *Needlepoint Designs from Oriental Rugs*, Charles Scribner's Sons (New York), 1981

Weiss, Rita and **Fontana**, Frank, *Miniature Iron-on Transfer Patterns*, Dover Publications (New York), 1979

HISTORICAL

Art Institute of Chicago, *Miniature Rooms: The Thorne Rooms at the Art Institute of Chicago*, Abbeville Press (New York), 1983

Stewart-Wilson, Mary, *Queen Mary's Dolls' House*, The Bodley Head, 1988

INTERIOR DECORATION

Wilhide, Elizabeth, *William Morris Decoration and Design*, Pavilion, 1991

Suppliers (Mail Order)

Many of these suppliers also exhibit their work at minatures fairs and sell through dolls' house shops.

'Cat.' indicates a catalogue is available. All prices are correct at time of going to press.

Please enclose a SAE with any enquiry where no catalogue is available.

Anglesey Dolls' Houses
Stanley Building
Stanley Street
Holyhead
Anglesey LL65 1HL
Cat. £1.50. Plans, kits and assembled.

Domat Designs
3 Lacy Road
London SW15 1NH
Cat. 2 x 1st class stamps. Kits and assembled.

Gable End Designs
190 Station Road
Knowle
Solihull
W. Midlands B93 0ER
Cat. 3 x 1st class stamps. Plans, kits, assembled and to commission; also Aga kit.

Lawrie Green
Westwood
Down Barton Road
St Nicholas at Wade
Birchington
Kent CT7 0PZ
Cat. large SAE. Plans (*see*** also Lighting).**

Honeychurch Toys Ltd
Woodlands
Ledge Hill
Market Lavington
Wilts SN10 4NW
Cat. £2.50. Kits and assembled.

David Hunt Dollshouses
410 Hotwells Road
Bristol
Avon BS8 4NU
Cat. SAE. Plans, kits, assembled and to commission.

Kingsmead Miniatures
8 Ringwood Drive
Kingsmead
Leeds
W. Yorks LS14 1AP
Cat. £1. Kits and assembled; also doors, windows, mouldings, tiles and brick strip.

James Parker Crafts
3 Blenheim Street
Hebden Bridge
W. Yorks HX7 8BU
Cat. £1.50. Plans, kits, assembled and to commission.

Sid Cooke Dolls' Houses
Unit 1
Millsborough House
Ipsley Street
Redditch
Worcs B98 7AL
Cat. 50p plus A5 SAE. Kits and assembled houses and shops.

Small World Dolls' Houses
Unit 6
Ludlow Hill Road
West Bridgford
Notts NG2 6HF
Cat. SAE. Kits and assembled; also imported furniture and accessories.

The Dolls' House Emporium
Victoria Road
Ripley
Derbys DE5 3YD
Cat. free. Kits; also imported furniture and accessories.

Torbay Model Workshop
35 Preston Down Road
Paignton
Devon TQ3 2RR

Cat. £1.50. Kits and to commission.

Wansbeck Dolls' Houses
Cherry Lodge
Outwood Lane
Bletchingley
Surrey RH1 4LR
Cat. £2.50, refundable on first order over £25. Plans, kits, DIY materials, specialist tools and accessories.

Sunday Dolls
7 Park Drive
London SW14 8RB
Cat. of dressed dolls and kits £3; kit list £1. Doll kits, dress patterns and dressed porcelain dolls to order.

Valerie Warren
21 Heath Road
Glossop
Derbys SK13 9BA
Wooden-headed dolls with soft bodies.

World of My Own
18 London Road
Farningham
Kent DA4 0JP
Cat. £1.50. Doll kits and dressed dolls; also furniture

and gardens – cat. 3 x 1st class stamps.

TOOLS

Blackwells of Hawkwell
733–735 London Road
Westcliff-on-Sea
Essex SS0 9ST
Cat. SAE. Tools, furniture and house kits, windows, mouldings, furniture etc. UK distributors for Houseworks (*see* Furniture Kits).

Lectromatic
70 High Street
Bentley
Doncaster
S. Yorks DN5 0AT
Cat. £2.60 plus 50p p.& p. Tools, houses, kits, plans etc.

LIGHTING

Lawrie Green
(*see* Dolls' Houses, Plans and Kits)
Booklet £4.95 plus 55p p.& p. Fully comprehensive guide, *Lighting Your Dolls' House*, 110 pages. Alternative systems, complete guide to installation, stockists, tools, price guides, fittings etc.

W. Hobby Limited
(*see* Shops)

Wood 'n' Wool Miniatures
Yew Tree House
3 Stankelt Road
Silverdale
Carnforth
Lancs LA5 0RB
Cat. £2.50 Transformers, kits and period lamps. Booklet: *How to Electrify a Dolls' House Using Copper Tape*, £1 (payable in stamps). Video available, SAE for details.

ROOFING

Cairn Tiles
6 College Green
Bideford
Devon EX39 3JY
Cat. SAE. Tiles, roof ridging, chimneys etc. in lightweight fibre material in choice of colours.

CHIMNEYS

Terry Curran
27 Chapel Street
Mosborough
Sheffield
S. Yorks S19 5BT
Cat. £1. Ceramic chimneys and other builder's items; ceramic flagstones and floor tiles.

Rosscraft
7 Little Britain
Dorchester
Dorset DT1 1NN
Cat. SAE. Wooden chimneys in period styles (*see* page 169).

ARCHITECTURAL MOULDINGS

Borcraft Miniatures
8 Fairfax View
Scotland Lane
Horsforth
Leeds
W. Yorks LS18 5SZ
List SAE; cat. £3. Cornices, skirting boards, pediments etc.

Bryntor Miniatures
60 Shirburn Drive
Torquay
Devon TQ1 4HR
Fireplaces, ceiling roses, panels etc. in cast resin; also pottery and dolls' houses and shops to commission.

DOORS AND WINDOWS

Borcraft Miniatures
(see Architectural Mouldings)
Kits in period styles.

Stillmore Homes
28 Hilliat Fields
Drayton
Nr Abingdon
Oxon OX14 4JQ
List SAE. Doors, windows with etched or stained glass (*see* Gardens and Conservatories).

The Welsh Doll House
(*see* Shops)
Cat. 75p. Victorian and Georgian sash windows, doors etc. which can be painted to simulate wood.

FLOORING

Borcraft Miniatures
Wooden floorboards, pine, oak, mahogany in two widths. Kits in period style.

Terry Curran
(*see* Chimneys)

FURNITURE KITS

Barbara Anne Miniatures
(*see* Shops)
List SAE. Simple furniture kits in plain styles; country pine etc.

Blackwells of Hawkwell
(*see* Tools)
Minimundus colour cat.

£3.95. Period style furniture kits; over 60 kits, from Georgian to Biedermeyer.

BATHROOM FITTINGS

Ann Shepley Ceramic Design
20 Tilford Road
Farnham
Surrey GU9 8DL
Cat. £2. Bathroom sets and fittings.

Sussex Crafts
Hassocks House
Comptons Brow Lane
Horsham
W. Sussex RH13 6BX
Cat. £2. Kits for WC; also flooring, plumbing, guttering, sinks, ranges, coppers, etc.

HINGES AND HANDLES

John Hodgson
25 Sands Lane
Bridlington
N. Humberside YO15 2JG
List SAE. Brass hardware, silver and gilt candelabra etc. Fine furniture; also to commission.

WALL TILES

Ann Shepley Ceramic Design
(*see* Bathroom Fittings)
Ceramic tiles including William de Morgan designs

WALLPAPERS

Thames Valley Crafts
Mere House
Dedmere Road
Marlow
Bucks SL7 1PD
Cat. £3. Wallpapers (samples with catalogue); also shop kits and fittings, lighting, food, fruit and vegetables etc.

FIREPLACES, GRATES AND RANGES

Blockhouse Models
16 Quantock Road
Worthing
W. Sussex BN12 2HG
Cat. SAE. Kitchen ranges, grates, fenders, mantelpieces etc.; Bath hob grate.

Borcraft Miniatures
(*see* Architectural Mouldings)
Fireplaces and wooden kits.

NEEDLEWORK KITS

Patricia Borwick
Neptune House
Cut Mill
Bosham
W. Sussex PO18 8PS
List SAE. Cat. £3. Carpets and other kits on canvas and silk gauze; also finished work to museum standard.

Carol Black Miniatures
Sun Hill
Great Strickland
Penrith
Cumbria CA10 3DF
Cat. £2.50 includes £1 voucher. Miniature patchwork quilt and cushion kit comprises $1/4$in (6mm) metal template, tiny pins, extra fine needles and instructions. Very large range of British miniatures.

ACCESSORIES

Bits and Pieces
18 Countisbury Road
Norton
Stockton on Tees
Cleveland TS20 1PZ
Cat. 50p plus SAE. Gilt mounts etc., intended for jewellery making, for use as picture frames, ornaments, and so on.

GARDEN SUPPLIES

Barbara Anne Miniatures
(see Shops)

Carol Mann Ceramics
One Home Farm
Westhorpe
Southwell
Notts NG25 0NG
Cat. SAE. Porcelain, stoneware and earthenware pots and planters.

Georgina Steeds
85 Summerleaze Road
Maidenhead
Berks SL6 8ER
Cat. SAE. Plants for house and garden; decorative trellises, greenhouses and conservatories; also to commission.

Stillmore Homes
(*see* Doors and Windows)
Conservatories.

The Secret Garden
(*see* Shops)
Cat. £2.25. Everything for the miniature garden; also food.

METALWORK

Black Country Miniatures
63 Church Street
Halesowen
W. Midlands B62 9LQ
**Ironwork, balconies,
railings, conservatories,
leaded windows and
brassware.**

John Watkins
12 Biddel Springs
Highworth
Swindon
Wilts SN6 7BH
**Railings, balconies, spiral
stairs, gates and garden
furniture; also to
commission.**

FINE ART

Kenneth Bird
Cherry Hinton
Rectory Road
Deal
Kent CT14 9LU
**Watercolour paintings,
landscapes, seascapes etc.
House portraits to
commission.**

Helen Scott-Langley
11 Overhill Road
Cirencester
Glos GL7 2LG
Reproductions in gouache

**of old master paintings;
also to commission.**

Becky Saxe Falstein
37 The Copse
Fareham
Hants PO15 6EG
**Watercolour paintings.
Reproductions of works by
Charles Rennie Mackintosh
a speciality.**

Shops

Please check shop opening times before visiting, as many shops close for a whole or half day each week. Opening times also vary.

ENGLAND

London

Kristin Baybars
7 Mansfield Road
Gospel Oak Village
London NW3 2JD
071 267 0934

W. Hobby Limited
Knights Hill Square
London SE27 0HH
081 761 4244
Cat. £2.

The Dolls' House
29 The Market
Covent Garden
London WC2E 8RE
071 379 7243
Cat. £1.50.

The Singing Tree
69 New Kings Road
London SW6 4SQ
071 736 4527
Cat. £2.50.

Avon

The China Doll
31 Walcot Street
Bath BA1 5BN
0225 465849
Cat. free.

Bedfordshire

Upstairs Downstairs
13 High Street
Bedford
0234 218600

Berkshire

The Eton Dolls' House
44 High Street
Eton
0753 850200

Buckinghamshire

Amersham Dolls' House
13–14 Market Walk
23 Market Square
Old Amersham HP7 0DG
0494 431944

Cambridgeshire

Granta Miniatures
19 High Street
Linton
Cambridge CB1 6HS
0223 891218

Cheshire

Fiddly Bits
24 King Street
Knutsford WA16 6DW
0565 65119

Lovin' Givin'
86 Lower Fold
Marple Bridge
Stockport SK6 5DU
061 427 7460

Cumbria

Present Time
68 Main Street
Keswick CA12 5DX
07687 73035

Top Drawer
Fisher Street
Carlisle CA3 8RH
0228 512560

Devon

Dolls and Miniatures
54 Southside Street
The Barbican
Plymouth PL1 2LB
0752 663676
Cat. £4, refundable with purchase £20 or over.

Miniature Curios
59 High Street
Honiton EX14 8PW
0404 46499

Essex

Patricia's Dolls' Houses
119 Eastgate
Basildon SS14 1AG
0268 293169

Gloucestershire

Bridge House Gallery
Fairford Road
Lechlade GL7 3DL
0367 52457

Hertfordshire

Whites Miniature World
Unit 6
81/82 Akeman Street
Tring HP23 6AJ
0442 890049
(also museum)

Kent

The Dolls' House Shop
68 High Street
Rochester ME1 1JY
0634 831615/363054

The Secret Garden
14 The Corn Exchange
Lower Pantiles
Tunbridge Wells
Kent TN2 5TE
0892 514660

Lincolnshire

The Stamford Poste
18 Empingham Road
Stamford PE9 2RH
0780 826821
List SAE.

Norfolk

Barbara Anne Miniatures
7 Bagley's Court
Pottergate
Norwich
Norfolk NR2 1TW
0603 610807

Surrey

**Dorking Dolls' House
Gallery**
23 West Street
Dorking RH4 1BY
0306 885785
Cat. £3.50.

Sussex

The Mulberry Bush
9 George Street
Brighton BN2 1RH
0273 493781
Cat. £3; also specialist
supplier of books on dolls'
houses and miniatures.
Book cat. 50p in stamps.

The Dolls' House Corner

Warwick Lane
Worthing BN11 3DP
0903 211785

Tollgate Miniatures
Bosham Walk
Old Bosham
Nr Chichester
0243 572205

West Midlands

Jennifer's of Walsall
(part of Grangers' Models and
Crafts)
51 George Street
Walsall WS1 1RS
0922 23382
Cat. £2.95.

Wiltshire

Small Sorts
40 Winchester Street
Salisbury SP1 1HG
0722 337235

Worcestershire

Chris-A-Liz
86 New Road
Kidderminster DY10 1AE
0562 825466
Cat. £3.

Yorkshire

Miniature Scene of York

37 Fossgate
York YO1 2TF
0904 638265
Cat. £2.

SCOTLAND

Royal Mile Miniatures
154 Canongate
Royal Mile
Edinburgh EH8 8DD
031 557 2293
Cat. £2.50.

WALES

The Welsh Doll House
11 Brecon Road
Abergavenny
Gwent NP7 5UH
0875 859113

**NORTHERN
IRELAND**

Leisureworld
Queens Street
Belfast
0247 853306

**CHANNEL
ISLANDS**

Cabbages and Kings
Red House (behind the House

of Jerome)
St Brelade
Jersey
0534 45560

FRANCE

Poupée Tendresse
9 rue Poussin
75016 Paris
(1) 42 88 50 42

DOLLS' HOUSE AND MINIATURES MAGAZINES

Dolls House and Miniature Scene (bi-monthly, on general sale)
EMF Publishing
5 Cissbury Road
Ferring
W. Sussex BN12 6QJ
0903 506626

Dolls' House World
(bi-monthly, subscription)
Ashdown Publishing
Shelley House
104 High Street
Steyning
W. Sussex BN4 3RD
0903 815622

The Home Miniaturist
(bi-monthly, subscription)
Ashdown Publications
(*see* above)

The Miniatures Catalogue of Great Britain
Ashdown Publications
(*see* above)

International Dolls' House News (quarterly, subscription)
PO Box 154
Cobham
Surrey
KT11 2YE
0932 867938

The British Dolls' House Hobby Directory is an annually updated publication of approximately 116 pages, published in May each year; it contains the names and addresses of over 250 makers and suppliers of dolls' house miniatures, dolls' house fairs and shops, and gives subscription details of dolls' house magazines. It costs £3 plus a strong A5 SAE stamped for 250g from:

LDF Publications
25 Priory Road
Kew
Richmond
Surrey TW9 3DQ

Nutshell News
(monthly, subscription)
Kalmbach Miniatures Inc.
PO Box 1612
Waukesha
WI 53187
(414) 796 8776

Miniatures Catalog
(annual)
Published by Kalmbach Miniatures Inc. (*see* above)

OTHER USEFUL ADDRESSES

International Guild of Miniature Artisans (IGMA)
PO Box 71
Bridgeport
NY 13030
USA
Annual show held in New York in April.

Posh Specialtours
Chuck and Glenda Cavanaugh
8117 Cowichan Road
Blaine
WA 98230–9566   USA
Small group interest and hobby tours in England, Europe and California.

Dolls' House Holidays
Wells Cottage
204 Main Road
Milford
Stafford ST17 0UN
Holiday courses in dolls' house making etc., May-October and winter breaks.

Club de la Miniature Française
9 rue Poussin
75016 Paris
France
Miniature club and magazine.

MAKERS OF DOLLS' HOUSES AND FINE FURNITURE

Work by these makers is shown in this book, and all will work to commission (SAE with enquiry). Many other makers will also work to special commission – *see* Suppliers (page 162) or refer to **The British Dolls' House Hobby Directory** (*see* opposite).

DOLLS' HOUSES

Samuel Halfpenny (J. Neill Richardson)
Glen View
Llanhamlach
Brecon
Powys LD3 7YB

Longbarn Enterprises (Christopher Cole)
Low Mill
Bainbridge
Leyburn
N. Yorks DL8 3EF

Peter Mattinson
100 Stockton Lane
York
N. Yorks YO3 0BU

Mulvany & Rogers
2 South Lane
Kingston-upon-Thames
Surrey KT1 2NJ

Mike Powell (LM Miniatures)
PO Box 91754
W. Vancouver
British Columbia V7V 4S1
Canada

Gordon Rossiter (Rosscraft)
7 Little Britain
Dorchester
Dorset DT1 1NN

Rudeigin Beag
Strawberrybank Cottage
Backmuir of Liff
by Dundee
Tayside DD2 5QU

Keith Thorne
12 Wades Road
Filton
Bristol
Avon BS12 7EE

Bernardo Traettino
33 Hertford Avenue
East Sheen
London SW14 8EF

Gary Ward (Wrenworthshire Homes)
6 Berners Street
off Petersen Road
Wakefield
W. Yorks WF1 4DY

Ellie Yannas
36 Westbridge Road
London SW11 3PW

FINE FURNITURE

John Davenport
Appledore
211 Botley Road
Burridge
Hants SO3 7BJ

Geoffrey Wonnacott
12 Ford Crescent
Bradworthy
Holsworthy
Devon EX22 7QR

METRIC CONVERSION TABLE

INCHES TO MILLIMETRES AND CENTIMETRES
MM – MILLIMETRES   CM – CENTIMETRES

Inches	MM	CM	Inches	CM	Inches	CM
1/8	3	0.3	9	22.9	30	76.2
1/4	6	0.6	10	25.4	31	78.7
3/8	10	1.0	11	27.9	32	81.3
1/2	13	1.3	12	30.5	33	83.8
5/8	16	1.6	13	33.0	34	86.4
3/4	19	1.9	14	35.6	35	88.9
7/8	22	2.2	15	38.1	36	91.4
1	25	2.5	16	40.6	37	94.0
1 1/4	32	3.2	17	43.2	38	96.5
1 1/2	38	3.8	18	45.7	39	99.1
1 3/4	44	4.4	19	48.3	40	101.6
2	51	5.1	20	50.8	41	104.1
2 1/2	64	6.4	21	53.3	42	106.7
3	76	7.6	22	55.9	43	109.2
3 1/2	89	8.9	23	58.4	44	111.8
4	102	10.2	24	61.0	45	114.3
4 1/2	114	11.4	25	63.5	46	116.8
5	127	12.7	26	66.0	47	119.4
6	152	15.2	27	68.6	48	121.9
7	178	17.8	28	71.1	49	124.5
8	203	20.3	29	73.7	50	127.0

ABOUT THE AUTHOR

Jean Nisbett began to take notice of period houses, their decoration and furniture before she was 10 years old, and they have been a consuming passion ever since. While bringing up a family she turned this interest to the miniature scale, and restored, decorated and furnished many dolls' houses. Her collection has been shown on Channel 4 television.

She began writing while working in the London offices of an American advertising agency, and is well-known as the leading British writer in the dolls' house field. Her articles have appeared regularly in the specialist miniatures and dolls' house magazines for over eight years, as well as in home decoration magazines. Jean Nisbett lives in Bath.